BLARNEY CASTLE

The seal of the Lord of Muskerry (after Crofton Croker 1824). [© British Library. All rights reserved.

BLARNEY CASTLE

Its History, Development and Purpose

Mark Samuel and Kate Hamlyn

CORK UNIVERSITY PRESS

First published in 2007 by
Cork University Press
Youngline Industrial Estate
Pouladuff Road
Togher
Cork
Ireland

British Library Cataloguing in Publication Data
A CIP catalogue record for this book is available from the British Library.

ISBN 978-1-85918-411-0

Typesetting by Red Barn Publishing, Skeagh, Skibbereen, Co. Cork
Printed by W. & G. Bairds Limited, Antrim, Northern Ireland

www.corkuniversitypress.com

This publication has received support from the Heritage Council under the 2007 Publications Grant Scheme.

Contents

List of Figures

Preface

Blarney Castle is one of the most popular tourist attractions in Ireland, with over 300,000 visitors a year. The majority come to kiss the Blarney Stone, and until recently the castle was seen as little more than the setting for the stone. The recent growth of leisure and affluence has resulted in a greater interest in archaeology and history of all kinds and a desire to understand how the past 'fits together'. This book is aimed at the visitor who wishes to understand the castle as a building and to learn more about its role in Irish history.

Blarney Castle is technically a 'tower house', a form of building much favoured by Irish clans in the late middle ages. At its simplest it consists of a number of large single chambers placed one on top of the other in a tower. It is very different from the motte and bailey and courtyard castles that tended to predominate in feudalised Europe, which most people are familiar with from literature and films. This book seeks, *inter alia,* to unpick this connection and to set Blarney firmly in its Gaelic tradition. To this end, the authors are very much indebted to the works of Dr Katharine Simms and Kenneth Nicholls, who have studied the Irish sources to increase our understanding of Gaelic clan life and elucidated it to those of us who have no Irish.

Much has been written on Blarney Castle over the years, but it has mostly been available only to those with an appetite for articles in antiquarian journals. The authors gained familiarity with the subject through Mark Samuel's PhD on tower houses. This thesis dealt with little-known ruined tower houses in West Cork, far from Blarney, although eventually the study area extended eastwards as far as Kilcrea Castle.

Mark first visited Cork in 1958, arriving in a carrycot in an Aer Lingus Dakota and being driven immediately to Rosscarbery. Despite visiting West Cork at least once a year since then, it was 2003 before he found the time to visit Blarney with his co-author and their sons. Blarney was a startling haven of beauty, peace and historical fascination, but there was little easily available information to satisfy the authors' curiosity about the place. What facts were available were liberally mixed with speculation and fancy.

This relative dearth of information inspired Mark to undertake a survey of the building in order to understand the sequence of construction and alteration, which would also describe how the rooms were used at different periods. However, parallel research provided more information about the Mac Carthy Muskerry clan than had been anticipated and these stories suggested that a description of Gaelic clan life and the Mac Carthy Muskerry clan in particular would bring life to the account of the castle. It would also help a visitor to understand why Irish castles or tower houses are distinct from feudal castles elsewhere. Ireland has these feudal castles too, for example King John's castle in Carlingford, Co. Louth, which inspired Kate Hamlyn when she visited it with her grandmother.

Once these additional themes had been included it appeared that something more than an article for an academic journal might emerge from the research. A book was planned, and then expanded to include the castle's life after the Mac Carthys departed. Dealing with its evolution into a tourist attraction involved dipping a toe into the churned-up waters of cultural history. Writing this book has been difficult since neither of the authors is an historian by training or has much knowledge of Irish. We have therefore relied heavily on secondary sources to provide a necessarily simplified account of Irish history. We cannot hope to please everyone, but have tried to avoid taking up any contentious positions in areas in which we recognise we are not qualified to hold them! Our aim has been to concentrate on giving a broad outline of events, to show the roles played by the Mac Carthy Muskerry clan and the Jefferyes and Colthursts within their times.

The Mac Carthy Muskerry clan was written about frequently in Victorian and Edwardian learned journals, but there has been no complete treatment of the family since 1922. Despite its detailed discussion of the family, this book does not pretend to be a family history of either the Mac Carthy Muskerry or the Jefferyes or the Colthursts. Inevitably, Blarney and its owners were affected by the Reformation, the Nine Years War, the Cromwellian invasion, the events of 1688, the Industrial Revolution, the Romantic Movement, the railway age, the Famine and the Civil War. It is the interweaving of these external events with the lives of the outstanding individuals from these families, living in this castle and its lands, which this book seeks to highlight.

Acknowledgements

We are indebted to Sir Charles Colthurst, the present owner of Blarney Castle, for allowing free access to the castle for survey and for the interest he has taken in the research and the materials he has provided (which he had previously assembled for his own studies). Brian Gabriel of the Blarney Historical Society provided valuable advice and email addresses. John Mulcahy, a knowledgeable local historian, also of the Blarney Historical Society, generously gave us access to his work in progress and exchanged emails with us on various topics. Dr Katharine Simms, on whose work so much of this book relies, kindly dealt with queries about Irish bards at the eleventh hour. Joanna Finnegan of the National Library of Ireland provided digital images of old Blarney views while waiving the rights fee.

We much appreciate the cooperation of various libraries, often at short notice, and would like to thank especially the staff at University College Cork, the Cork Archive, Cork City Library, the Society of Antiquaries of London and the British Library. Emma Poynton of the Office of Public Works Library in Dublin also searched out information on our behalf. The staff at Ramsgate

Public Library helped with our endless requests for inter-library loans of obscure articles and apparently tedious books, despite the library burning down in August 2004 (nearly taking one of our inter-library loans with it).

Mark Samuel's 1998 PhD thesis was the foundation on which this book was written. Thanks are therefore due for their past support, insight and criticisms to Professor James Graham-Campbell of the Institute of Archaeology at University College London, who supervised the thesis, and Dr Tom McNeill of Queen's University Belfast, who rigorously examined it.

Our sons, Ned and Fineen, deserve our thanks for having developed the ability to allow their parents time to work uninterrupted.

A dual authorship has worked very well, in that one author plants excessively while the other reaps (or pulls up!). It is hoped that this approach has resulted in the right balance being struck in this book.

MWS

KLH

Ramsgate, April 2006

CHAPTER 1

Where is Blarney Castle?

THE BLARNEY STONE is famous all over the world; the idea of 'blarney' is closely associated with foreign stereotypes of Irishness. But if you ask someone without an Irish background whether they know about Blarney Castle, the response is often a blank look. This highlights the fact that one tiny part of the castle has become so significant that it can be divorced from its context to the extent that many people are not aware of the castle's existence.

Looking at Blarney Castle, a visitor might imagine that the life and habits of its lord would have been much like those of the feudal leaders whose castles we are familiar with from films like *Robin Hood*. Although there are similarities, Gaelic lordship and Irish clan culture were very different from the primogeniture-based, land-holding feudal system common elsewhere in Europe at the time.

This book seeks to illuminate the context in which the Blarney Stone sits. It deals with the history of the area around Blarney; the Gaelic society that built the castle; the function of the Castle, first for the Mac Carthy clan, then for its subsequent owners; the gradual development of the property and finally its development as one of Ireland's major tourist destinations.

The area of Co. Cork in which Blarney Castle stands was once known as Muskerry. It was then a discrete area within the county, although this is not apparent to the modern visitor. There are no 'Welcome to Muskerry' signs and its natural boundaries of rock, river and marsh are easily crossed nowadays. However, these natural barriers made the area easy to defend in the Middle Ages and Muskerry was thus a desirable territory for the Mac Carthy clan.

The map in Figure 1 is derived from a map made in about 1600 for the *Pacata Hibernia* (Stafford 1896) which shows the main features of the area. It gives an indication of how different things were then. Transport was very difficult: there were no roads, only tracks, and much of the land was still covered in forest. Nothing apart from tower houses and churches now survives in the landscape to give a clue to the nature and intensity of Gaelic rural settlement. The main settlement was the island community of Cork City, and the only convenient route through the territory was along the valley of the River Lee. Travelling up the Lee, one left the Anglicised culture and commercial centre of the city and passed through a gently undulating vale of fine

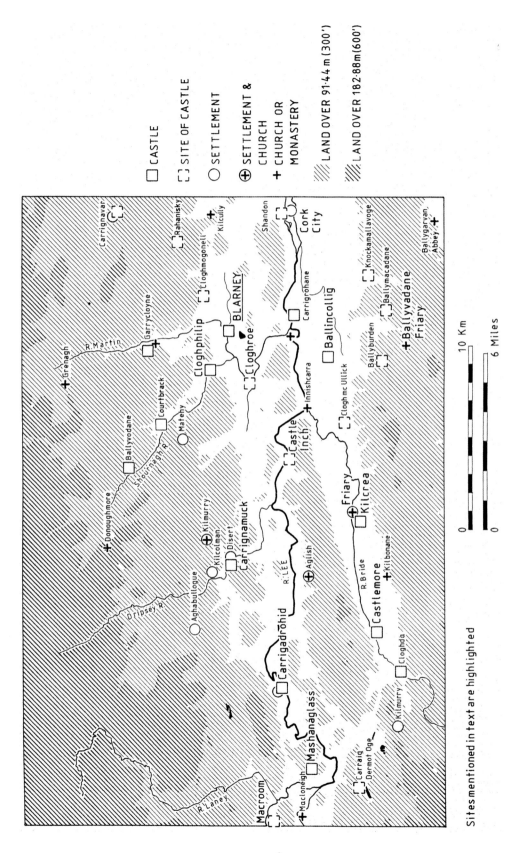

Fig. 1 Map showing the settlement of east Muskerry c. 1600; based on Pacata Hibernia and other sources (after Stafford 1896). [Ordnance Survey Ireland Permit No. 8372 © Ordnance Survey of Ireland and Government of Ireland]

farmland. Going westward into the ever emptier and wilder landscape of West Cork, a traveller would finally reach the mountains that hug Gouganebarra Lake, and the shrine of St Finbarr, one of the most sacred sites of Co. Cork. Muskerry included the Lee valley and its tributaries, the lands bordering these and the hills that slope northwards to the River Blackwater.

Blarney is situated in an area immediately to the north of Cork City where several tributaries of the Lee meet to form a sheltered, well-watered valley. The tower house was built on a low spur or promontory of rock projecting beneath the water meadows of the lush valley. The Com-abhan (Comeen, 'crooked stream') meets the River Martin just east of the castle to form what is now called the Blarney River. They run west to join the Shournagh River, which in its turn flows through a cleft in the hills to join the River Lee.

Blarney Castle is nowadays the most famous of the Mac Carthy Muskerry tower houses and was the favourite home of the chieftain for much of its history; but it was not strategically important in the manner that Windsor Castle was to the King of England. It was not always the chieftain's castle and fell out of favour after 1620. Its site was in fact relatively peripheral to Muskerry and had only been in Mac Carthy hands for a few years when the castle was built. Its importance was that it controlled a natural route to Cork City and thus presented many interesting possibilities for the clan.

An important fact to note about Blarney is that during the Middle Ages it was at the very edge of English rule in Ireland, and later, during the sixteenth and seventeenth centuries, it was in an area much favoured for English settlement. This proximity to a different culture made it necessary for the Mac Carthy Muskerry chieftains to be 'bilingual' in both speech and legal matters. As a result, there is a relative wealth of documentation compared with contemporary clans in areas more remote from English rule and the Common Law. While in no way pretending to be an in-depth technical treatment, this book draws together these published but little-known sources (the majority dating to before 1920) to serve as a general introduction to the 'late' Gaelic culture that existed in Munster and the circumstances that led to its demise.

CHAPTER 2

Gaelic Society in the Late Medieval Period

WHILE MUCH OF Western Europe was living under a feudal system in the Middle Ages, Gaelic society retained many ancient Celtic features. Celtic societies had gradually disappeared across Europe with Roman invasion, the imposition of the Roman Empire and the upheavals and migrations that followed the decline of that empire. Ireland, by virtue of its geography, had escaped most of this and thus retained a very different social and legal system.

The most important unit of Gaelic society was the family or clan. By 1400 the most important clans, such as the Mac Carthys, had developed into a distinctive group of administrators and landowners who came to dominate other families in the same territory. An individual's status was dictated by the importance of their clan, and status within a clan was in turn dictated by whether one was a member of the ruling family or not.

The chieftain

Each clan was ruled by the *taoiseach* (chieftain). *Tiernacht* or '*tierna*' and '*ban-tierna*' (Bennett 1869, p. 124) seem to have been the terms used for the chieftain and his wife in the sixteenth century. Eligibility to become a clan chieftain was restricted to those members of the clan descended from a chieftain. (This pattern is also found in non-European cultures.) This group was called the *derbfine* (ruling lineage). While feudal society usually provided a single obvious candidate to inherit power, whether a king or a baron, the Gaelic system potentially provided a large pool of men from which a chieftain could be chosen. A disadvantage was that after four generations the system began to fragment and younger sons often began to form sub-families or septs who had to find their own lands. The *derbfine*'s security lay in the fact that no one else in the clan could inherit the chieftainship. They could freely give positions of power and trust to other clan members, knowing that these men would be unable to challenge them for leadership. Rivalry was thus concentrated within their family group.

The chieftain was chosen by a system of election within the *derbfine* (Nicholls 1993a, p. 423). The sons, nephews and cousins of a chieftain formed a group called *righdhamhna* ('king material') and would all be eligible for a turn as chieftain. Second in prestige was the *tánaiste* (tanist). On the chieftain's death, the tanist became chieftain and a new tanist would emerge from the *righdhamhna.* This system had the advantage that the tanist would be of proven competence – he would usually be middle-aged or even elderly when he became chieftain, and his chieftainship might be short but long enough for a new tanist to get experience. It was thus possible for a series of peaceable successions to occur through simple seniority.

While father-to-son succession was unusual, it was occasionally possible. When it occurred in the Mac Carthy clan over two or three generations the English administration was beguiled into thinking that the family was conforming to English law and custom. As we will see, the chieftain was quite happy to play along with this idea when it was convenient. The smooth succession of sons demonstrates the exceptional grip of the Muskerry chieftain on his clan. The chieftainship was a demanding job: chieftains rarely abdicated and usually died in harness. Very unusually in 1583 an older man, Callaghan Mac Teige, voluntarily made way for his younger nephew, Cormac Mac Dermod, but was compensated with another castle.

Tanists were sometimes challenged by a rival in the *derbfine;* the act of seizing power by whatever means was usually taken as proof of suitability for chieftainship. A cynical English observer stated that 'he that hath strongyst armye and hardest swyrde among them hath best right and tytill' (Simms 1987, p. 51–2). Murder of the tanist was frowned upon, however, and it is recorded that when the Mac Carthy Muskerry chieftain was murdered by another member of the *derbfine* in 1494 the murderer was subsequently disqualified from becoming chieftain and the chieftainship passed instead to the murdered man's son. Earlier in Irish history, a successful rival might blind or castrate the official tanist to make him unsuitable for the chieftaincy. The aggressor would not be automatically disqualified by the *brehons* (councillors and judges to the clan, see below) from becoming chieftain. Although lineage killing was disapproved of, after 1494 there were a number of Mac Carthys who became chieftains despite having committed this crime.

An important form of social control within the clan was the maintenance of 'face'. Gaelic society was brutally realistic about power relationships, with none of the comfortable fictions of love and fealty adopted in the feudal world to mask coercion. A successful lord would sometimes require a defeated rival to accept gifts, not out of goodwill but to underline his abasement. Generosity and hospitality were highly valued in Gaelic society but could be used tactically. A chieftain had to be seen to be imposing his will on others and reckless impetuous bravery was seen as the highest virtue. Chivalry was less valued.

On the death of the chieftain, no lands were bequeathed to any individual. The clanlands were instead redistributed among the members of the noble family, who all moved up one place in the pecking order. At the same time the co-heirs (all male issue of the father) would make a new partition of the lands, favouring themselves, their relatives and favourites. Women could not inherit. In Munster the partition of the lands was made by the most senior clan member, who could take the best portion for himself (Nicholls 1993a, p. 432). This may have contributed to stability.

The chieftain's yearly round

Although the tower houses adopted by the Irish chieftains look imposing, and certain towers were allocated to particular high-ranking members of the *derbfine*, there was a deep-rooted prejudice against static headquarters. A chieftain lived on the move. He hunted, feasted, raided and fought in the open air; serious differences were resolved by battles and raids, not sieges, which were common in the feudal system. When Irish clans were involved in warfare, they typically went to their 'fastnesses', inaccessible mountainous or forested places where they could hide out for long periods, rather than retreat to towers.

The *aimser chue* ('coshering season') was between New Year's Day and Shrovetide (Simms 1978, p. 79). This was when vassals paid their traditional dues to the chieftain, usually by providing hospitality and accommodation for him and his retinue for a number of days, dictated by custom. This was a lean time of year, when it was most convenient for the chieftain to have others feed his followers. A vassal might be called upon to feed the lord and his followers twice or even four times a year for two consecutive days and nights. The expense of the *cuid oidhche* would be to the value of six beef bullocks (ibid., p. 81). A sixteenth-century writer, Richard Stanihurst, recorded the Irish nobles at

> [a] set feast, which they call coshering, whereto flock all theyr retayners, whom they name followers, their rithmours (Rhymers), their bardes, theyr harpers that feede them with musicke, and when the harper twangeth or singeth a songe, all the company must be whist (attend) [. . .] In their coshering they sit on straw, they are served on straw, and lie on mattresses and pallets of straw. (Ibid.)

The purpose of these tours was not simply idle pleasure. The Mac Carthy Muskerry would use such visits to resolve disputes and confirm successions among vassal clans. In about 1592, for example, an assembly of the chief men of Muskerry elected Amhlaoibh O Leary as the chieftain of the O Learys. Cormac Mac Dermot Mor, lord of Muskerry, would in such an instance present the new O Leary chieftain with a 'white rod of office' to confirm the succession (Ó Murchadha 1985, p. 208). The O Learys no doubt provided a rich feast on that occasion.

Creaght (cattle raiding), a major feature of ancient Celtic life to judge from the literature and mythology (the *Tain*, etc.), had become largely obsolete by the end of the sixteenth century. However, it suddenly underwent a modest revival among the great magnates of Munster in the unstable conditions of the time. Such forays were a sort of psychological warfare to deter rival overlords from asserting claims over the fringes of a 'sphere of influence'. Cattle raids seem to have become a princely sport – raids on Tipperary herds were organised by the first Earl of Clancarthy (Cronnelly 1864, p. 261) who invited his vassal chieftains to join him, as if inviting them to an important fox hunt.

Compared with that in other parts of Gaelic Ireland, the population of Muskerry was relatively static and there was only one recorded cattle raid in the period. The last recorded instance of such a raid was in 1600, when Mac Carthy Riabhach raiders killed some O Leary men while stealing their cattle. On this occasion, the O Learys' protector, Mac Carthy Muskerry, was bound to act, but the President of Munster refused him permission to deal with the offenders in the traditional way.

Some alien clans had been 'swallowed whole' by Muskerry power – the Learys, Mahonys, Healeys, Hurleys, Longs and Cronins (ibid.; and see Fig. 2). They owed allegiance, certain services and payments, but were otherwise left pretty much to their own devices as freeholders.

Sub-septs

Inevitably, after about four generations, with population growth, the *dearbfine* would begin to fragment into competing septs. While still adhering to the chieftain, they would perhaps begin to consider their sept as of equal importance to the ruling group. A competition for the chieftainship might then occur. Only two such struggles occurred amongst the Mac Carthys during Blarney's period as an Irish stronghold, modest in comparison with some Irish clans. The involvement of the Lordship of Ireland (the English Crown's representatives) in later disputes meant that recourse was made to legal solutions, at the expense of the clan's identity and coherence but with less bloodshed.

When a sept split off from the *derbfine* a patronymic 'tag' would distinguish it from the main lineage. This usually derived from some nickname of the new founding father of the sept, such as Riabhach ('swarthy') or Laidir ('powerful'). Such offshoots tended to weaken the main clan and the Mac Carthy Muskerrys discouraged them by restricting their access to clan lands. However, the six 'Septs of the Carties in Muskrie' enjoyed the rights of freeholders and held no less than 66 ploughlands in 1600 (Butler 1910, p. 127).

Although lands were important, the chieftain ruled by prestige rather than by direct land ownership (see above). The chieftain directly only held a small parcel of the clanlands for life. Here he would have his house or hall. This traditional society was not a cash economy. Cash was obtained in the course of trade but was of little use except for buying foreign luxuries such as wine (Simms 1978, p. 67). Until the latter half of the sixteenth century no one owned anything in the sense we now understand, apart from personal items and clothing. Cattle were an important sign of wealth, but most important were the dues owing to the chieftain. The exactions a chief could make from his people were the true measure of his status. When it came to relations with other clans, no lord ever admitted that another was his equal.

Marriage and the role of noblewomen

Romantic love was not thought to be a necessary component of marriage: girls of good family were 'preferred' to good husbands and had no say in the matter. Distance was no object when it came to an advantageous marriage. One Mac Carthy chieftain, Sir Cormac Mac Teige, the fourteenth Lord, married a daughter of the Butler family of Tipperary (Collins 1954; no. 1, p. 2 *JCHAS*). His

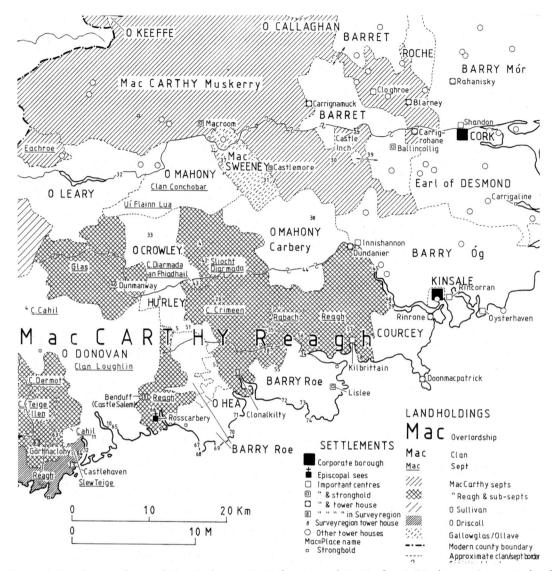

Fig 2 Political map of central Co. Cork c. 1570 (after Samuel 1998, fig. c) [Ordnance Survey Ireland Permit No. 8372 © Ordnance Survey of Ireland and Government of Ireland]

will indicates that the marriage to Joan Butler was in essence a series of verbal agreements about property between two families which were made in public at the church door rather than a religious service within the church as today (Gillman 1892b, p. 196). He gave her leave to remarry on his death subject to certain legal niceties.

Daughters left fatherless, such as the daughters of Sir Cormac Mac Teige, were the responsibility of their uncle(s). The same very interesting will shows that Sir Cormac appointed his brother to find husbands for his three daughters by his second marriage, Ellyne, Gilley and Mary ny Cormac. These girls would have lived at Blarney until marriage (possibly in the room traditionally identified as the Young Ladies' Chamber).

The chieftain's wife had considerable administrative responsibilities and status and was her husband's representative when he was not available, as well as being the mistress of the castle and holder of the keys. No stranger could be admitted while the chieftain was away. Like her husband, the chieftain's wife and her retinue could demand free ingress and entertainment in the house of any vassal at all hours (Gillman 1892a, p. 35). Chieftains' wives sometimes built their own castles (Lee 1914, p. 61, Ó Murchadha 1985, p. 54) and occasionally they had to defend them.

Despite their importance, wives could be 'set aside' at will should the chieftain care to remarry, as Sir Cormac Mac Teige did in 1570. He subsequently claimed in his will that his first wife was already married at the time he 'used' her (Gillman 1892b, p. 196) and thus dispossessed his son and daughter by that marriage. The lack of stigma attached to illegitimacy and the ease of remarriage meant that the *derbfine* continually expanded. This expansion could only be supported by taking lands from other, weaker land-owning clans or collateral septs.

Members of the *derbfine* as a rule always married out. A surviving pedigree of a minor Mac Carthy sept (the Clann Taidhg Ruaidh na Scairte) shows a pattern of constant intermarriage with the other septs in West Cork (Ó Murchadha 1994, p. 38). The opportunity to forge alliances with other major Cork families contributed to the relative stability of the province. Between 1603 and 1641 intermarriage occurred freely between the important families of Cork, whether they were Irish clans, old established English families or wealthy new settler families. The Mac Carthy Muskerrys even sought the hands of the daughters of staunch Protestants such as the immensely rich Sir Richard Boyle. Boyle's diary hints at the religious fortitude he displayed in turning down such tempting offers (MacCarthy-Morrogh 1986, p. 276).

In contrast to their brothers, who seemed to be christened with a very limited (and thus confusing) range of names, girls were permitted a wide variety of attractive names deriving from romances, such as Honora or Margaret. Like those of their brothers, their name was always accompanied by that of their father, for example Ellen ni Cormac (Ellen, daughter of Cormac).

The ollamh (ollaves; learned and professional class)

The Mac Carthys employed a number of other families, such as the Learys, Sweeneys and Collinses, to carry out specialist functions such as bards or doctors. The Mac Egans were hereditary *britheam* (lawyers) of the Mac Carthy Muskerry (Butler 1910, p. 127). They were the most important of the ollaves because social behaviour was not dictated by written law. Instead there was a vast body of tradition and precedent governing the smallest detail of duties owed by one family to another. These rules were so intricate that no one individual could be expected to remember them all, nor could they be codified into a general system of law. These *brehons,* usually an hereditary role, were the repositories and interpreters of tradition who would advise the chieftain and tanist on the correct course of action. A modern example of this system is found in the family of Nelson Mandela who acted as advisers and councillors to the Xhosa king in much the same way.

The O'Lynes acted as physicians and surgeons (Ó Murchadha 1985, p. 217) while the O'Dalys were 'rhymers' or bards. The broad class called bard included authors, reciters and musical performers. The O'Donins were the Mac Carthy's chroniclers and were presumably more rigorously factual than the bards. However, the last official poet of the MacCarthys was Tadhg Ó Duinnín and his laments written after the loss of Blarney to the English survive (ibid., p. 139; see also Ch. 7).

Each professional family enjoyed a portion of freehold lands as support (Butler 1910, p. 127). Other branches of the same families performed the same role for other chieftains. A member of the O'Lynes was even recorded as practising in Spain (Ó Murchadha 1985, p. 217).

While some might question this, it is realistic to class the clergy among the professional classes who relied on the favour of the Mac Carthy Muskerry. The castle of Blarney would have had a chaplain. The name Noonan had long been associated with a variety of ecclesiastical posts, and it is probable that Sir William Noynyn, priest, who witnessed the will of Cormac Mac Teige Mac Carthy (the fourteenth lord) in 1583, was the chaplain of Blarney (ibid., p. 198). The O'Herlihy family had a similar long-standing connection with the church and produced the saintly Thomas O'Herlihy, who was appointed Bishop of Ross in 1561 and was one of only three Irish bishops to attend the Council of Trent (ibid., p. 189). The Blessed Thaddeus Mac Carthy was appointed Bishop of Ross in 1482 but his ministry was frustrated at every turn by the Desmonds, who did not like others to appoint the Bishop of Ross and would not have chosen a Mac Carthy.

The chaplain probably enjoyed the use of a chapel in the vicinity of the castle, perhaps the one mentioned in 1702 (MacCarthy 1990, p. 162). There was apparently a small chapel within the castle itself (Ch. 10).

The gallóglaigh (gallowglas) and Ceithearn Tige

The major clans increasingly relied on families of professional mercenaries, gallowglas, for fighting. The leading gallowglas clan for the Mac Carthys was the Mac Sweeneys, who played an important role in Muskerry. The chieftain placed a high degree of trust in these individuals: on one occasion a gallowglas was appointed as the chieftain's executor and guardian of his heir. The Sweeneys enjoyed their own lands in Muskerry, complete with their own castles (Fig. 2).

When the chieftain was in residence the door normally stood open, but no visitor escaped the surveillance of the hereditary Mac Sweeney gallowglas guard. The name of one of their commanders, Donell McOyn illoyghey (an locha) survives in Cormac Mac Teige's 1583 will. His function is described as 'keeping and guard of the castle [. . .] within the grate' (Gillman 1892b, p. 197). The grate is the yett or grating which was housed in the main doorway at Blarney. The castles were also guarded by the *ceithearn tighe*, who formed the castle garrisons, which came to play an important role in an increasingly militarised Gaelic society. The context makes it clear that security within and without the castle was shared between different officers, the grate being the frontiers of their territories.

The common people and their role

It must be understood that no area in Muskerry was occupied exclusively by members of a single sept or even a single clan; the population also included 'follower septs' who blended loosely into the dominant clan – the O'Riordans, O'Morohoes, Clancallaghans and MacSweeneys (Butler 1910, p. 127). These groupings held no land but were retainers of the lord and supported on his own desmesne lands or at the expense of the freeholders. The ceithearn tige, the castle garrison, tended to be composed of members of the follower septs. Remoter castles such as Macroom and Mashanaglas were entrusted to a gallowglas, Donell Mac Sweeney (Gillman 1892c, p. 199), who presumably ran their full-time wards.

Although the economic position of these groupings was particularly weak, unlike the feudal peasants of England and elsewhere they could migrate freely and did not form a stable population settled on the land (Ellis 1985, p. 44). The precarious position of the churl can be overstated; even the weakest members of society could, in principle, call upon the protection of their overlord if slighted by another lord. There is an apocryphal tale of an old woman who lived in an area contested between two families. She gave a loaf to the follower of a great lord but refused to give a second loaf, because that would step outside the obligations of normal hospitality. She then threatened the man with punishment from her protector, the great lord's worst enemy (Simms 1978, p. 78).

We are unlikely to know the name of a person of this class, unless they be male and a soldier. The hundreds of fiants and pardons generated by the unrest of the late sixteenth century name such unimportant individuals and thereby hint at the very mixed composition of the population of Muskerry at that time. In general these people, like the inferior members of the clan, had no rights and little control of the 'election' of chieftains or the disposal of lands. Despite this, they remained remarkably loyal to the end of the period of Gaelic society. The call of the chieftain for a 'rising out' raised large forces even in the struggles of the late seventeenth century, when he was technically no more than a landlord.

The semi-nomadic nature of life and the ephemeral nature of poor people's homes means that little is known about Gaelic rural settlement, but there is a growing appreciation of its regional variations (Nicholls 1993a, p. 404). Much of Gaelic Ireland practised pastoralism; however, the fact that in Muskerry both corn and cattle were targeted for destruction by the English in 1601 (Stafford 1896, pp. 214, 271) suggests a more settled rural economy. It is only by plotting the positions of churches, friaries and castles that it is possible to form an idea of the main distribution of settlement in Muskerry (Fig. 1). Maps published in English sources such as the *Pacata Hibernia* indicate that while some familiar nucleated settlements were in existence in 1600, the main clue to settlement concentration was the churches and castles plotted on the map. Permanent settlement was virtually absent above the 183m (600') contour line and most 'high status' buildings were in the river valleys.

Intensive agriculture seems to have been established in the neighbourhood of Rosscarbery by

1640, largely at the behest of the English settlers (Gillman 1895, pp. 1–20, *JCHAS*). However before this the common people probably practised the 'long-fallow system', in which the land was left untilled to pasture for several years between each sowing. This was probably more common than a regular course of crop rotation (Nicholls 1993a, p. 411). The recognition of these people in the landscape and their role in medieval Irish life must await further research and extensive excavation and publication.

Feudal influence on Ireland

The influence the Irish had on the customs of their conquerors is well known: it has often been said that the Norman families such as the Fitzgerald Earls of Desmond ended up becoming 'more Irish than the Irish'. Irish chieftains traditionally made alliances according to local advantage; there was no national sense of the Irish sticking together against the Normans. They lived as amicably with the Norman settlers as expedience allowed. Less frequently mentioned is the way that the English brought some influence to bear on Irish life by importing features of feudal society into the country. The Anglo-Norman feudal influence brought an increased emphasis on military lordship and the holding of land. The Mac Carthys and other important families became more clearly an elite group. Within the Mac Carthy clan, the *derbfine* gradually became less accountable to the body of the clan.

The English referred to their authority over Ireland as the Lordship of Ireland. While this concept embraced the whole of the country in principle, in practice Ireland was divided into an area which obeyed English and feudal law, chiefly the eastern side, and the Gaelic areas where Irish traditions continued unhampered. The English constantly tried to encourage Irish lords to abide by English law but its precepts and basis were so alien to Gaelic tradition that there was continuous conflict between the two. The Mac Carthy Muskerry chieftains who held Blarney Castle continually performed a tricky balancing act between the law of the two lands, but generally sought alliance with the Crown (Ellis 1985, p. 91).

In the medieval period large areas of western Europe, and indeed parts of Ireland under English rule, were run on feudal lines. The major difference between the feudal and the traditional Gaelic system was that in the feudal system all land was ultimately owned by the king, or equivalent ruler, and land which was held by the lower orders of nobility (barons, earls and so on) was held in exchange for duty. Some of these duties were military, such as the provision of knights ('knight service') for warfare; additionally their peasants could be called up as foot soldiers. Other duties could be converted into cash payments. Within the feudal system women could inherit lands and titles, but the primary transfer of wealth and power was to the eldest son (primogeniture). It was a world controlled by both legal documents and the exercise of military power. The existence of towns and a powerful king were vital to its successful operation. Feudalism was planted in England by the Normans and they created one of the most centralised and orderly kingdoms in Europe.

Ireland was one of the few places in Europe where the spread of feudalism was limited. The new order competed with a native social organisation that was incompatible in certain critical respects. The absence of the Common Law meant there was no primogeniture, and property could not be vested in the persons of female heiresses or under-age wards. However, by the end of the medieval period Gaelic society had taken on many of the customs of the English; this is illustrated by the transformation of Gaelic law that occurred between 1350 and 1500, during which the pledge, the jury and basic common-law concepts were adopted (Ellis 1985, p. 46). Inheritance, however, was still ruled by Irish traditions.

CHAPTER 3
Gaelic Tower Houses

ALTHOUGH BLARNEY IS known as a castle, it is fundamentally a tower house, an architectural form that differs from the style of castle favoured in feudal Europe. Tower houses are found all over Europe, particularly in Scotland (Cairns 1987, p. 10), Greece and in Italian cities. It is interesting to note that these were all places where feudal structures were weak or irrelevant.

The dating of tower houses is not a subject for the faint-hearted. The best-argued position is that the tower houses of Ireland were for the most part built in the fifteenth century, being particularly popular in the first half of that century (McNeill 1997, p. 203). The tower houses of Cork were therefore relative latecomers on the scene, developing in a regional tradition rather than being 'borrowed' from elsewhere (Samuel 1998, p. 199). The succession of structures at Blarney demonstrates this evolution.

In Ireland tower houses seem to have been favoured in areas where the Irish had recaptured land colonised by the Anglo-Normans. They were extremely popular in counties such as Tipperary and Limerick (and virtually absent from Ulster). These areas were fertile and after being regained often retained much of their manorial organisation and arable farming, though under Irish control. Areas of 'pure Gaelic' culture such as Ulster had little use for any sort of permanent secular building, probably because of the survival there of a more nomadic pastoral culture.

Nucleated settlement was unusual in the Gaelic areas of Ireland (Nicholls 1993a, p. 399); for example, in West Cork there is little certain evidence of urbanisation prior to 1600, except at Rosscarbery, Timoleague and Kinsale. Settlements are recorded as forming about castles (ibid., p. 404) and the tower house encouraged nucleated settlement in a society where it was otherwise unusual (ibid., p. 399). The tower house could form a subsistence centre for intensive seasonal agricultural activity, such as apple and vegetable growing, as well as milling and other activities requiring close supervision (Cairns, 1987, p. 18). Hardly surprisingly, many tower houses now stand in farms. Certainly by the sixteenth century the tower house was forming part of a more permanently settled existence.

A sixteenth-century illustration of Carrickfergus shows the town surrounded by a penumbra of temporary Irish huts (ibid., Fig. 7:34). These temporary towns of wattled huts were built to provide additional housing outside castles elsewhere in Ireland (Simms 1978, p. 91) and temporary halls could also be built for special occasions (Mallory and McNeill 1991, p. 301). Much of the population was involved in a cycle of transhumance (Lucas 1989, pp. 58–9) and this discouraged investment in permanent structures. Originally tower houses were probably unoccupied for part of the year, especially when the chieftain went abroad with his entourage to enjoy the fruits of the 'coshering season' (Ch. 2; Simms 1978, p. 79). Later, as the addition of domestic features suggests, they became more important as permanent dwellings. By the time extensive records began to be kept a tower house was regarded as equivalent to a manor house (Samuel 1998, pp. 196–7).

Originally stone castles were introduced by the invading Normans. The Gaelic tower house form, developed about 200 years later seems to have been inspired by minor Norman strongholds, and was enthusiastically adopted by many Irish clans and Hiberno-Norman families; they proliferated in areas where the Lordship of Ireland held no direct control and attempted to rule through local magnates. Muskerry was just such an area. Tower houses were relatively sparse here compared with, say, Limerick; this may have been due to the strong central control of the Mac Carthy Muskerry.

Irish tower houses usually stand three to four floors high with a battlement around the top. They are normally oblong in plan but round, square or even trapezoid plans also occur. It was usual for at least one floor to be vaulted with a vast barrel vault. A spiral stair provided access to all floors. The design of tower houses is far more varied and complex than their external shape would suggest. Studies of tower houses are confirming that regional variants existed, much as regional architecture can be seen today.

Study of the tower houses of Cork shows that the internal layout became more elaborate with time. A distinct regional tradition of early tower houses built between about 1450 and 1510 has been recognised (Samuel 1998, p. 199). These simple buildings consisted of four large plain chambers stacked on top of each other. The windows were of minimal size and fireplaces were absent.

The unlit ground-floor room did not communicate with the remainder of the building. This was a security feature, sometimes further enhanced by a strong vaulted ceiling, which deterred attackers from burning the building from the inside. It is traditionally assumed that it was used for storage and was occasionally used as a refuge for any cattle in the vicinity during a raid. For example, in 1457 Ua Ruairc of Brefnei in Leitrim evaded a large raid by putting his 'flocks and herds into a keep' – *'do cur a caeraidheacht a n-daingen'* (Lucas 1989, p. 118); the word *'daingen'* generally suggests a tower (Kenneth Nicholls, pers. comm. Samuel 1998, p. 220).

The upper floors were entered through an opening several metres above the ground at first-floor level, which was reached by a ladder. This difficult access suggests these early tower houses were not intended for everyday use. The first and second floors were usually devoid of creature comforts, seemingly uninhabitable to modern eyes. The presence of latrines shows habitation, but the original role of the rooms cannot otherwise be determined. Perhaps these chambers never had a defined role, although they were well suited for storage. In time the first floor of Blarney was made relatively comfortable, but the ground-floor chamber lacks even a level floor.

The fourth floor of these early towers was usually provided with a stone floor supported by a barrel vault, and it was much larger and taller than the other chambers. The presence typically of a relatively large window in each wall and a latrine at the north-east (downwind) corner identifies these chambers as halls. A central hearth rather than a fireplace was favoured, and the smoke would escape through a louvre in the roof. The temporary inhabitants had very basic cooking requirements and needed no separate kitchen. A kitchen was eventually added at Blarney, and late tower houses always have such a chamber, recognisable by its huge fireplace.

A legend, presumably translated from the vernacular Gaelic in the nineteenth century, shows in what detail the memory of the hall of one Cork tower house, Ballynacariga Castle, was preserved. One evening the chieftain and his wife were confronted with the five secret sons she thought she had drowned at birth. The scene is set in their hall where

> oaken tables extended through the centre of the great hall, creaking under the weight of the beef and the huge baskets of bread which were piled upon them. Round the walls were ranged shelves, upon which were placed vessels of *usquebaugh* [whiskey] and the best *meiodh* [mead] of the Carberries; and at the head of the hall was another large table, at right angles with the others. Upon this were haunches of venison and tankards of claret for his principal guests. (Bennett 1869, p. 197)

Although the hall is not specifically mentioned, the translated elegy of Tadhg an dúna of Togher by the bard Donal na Tuile (1696) provides a vivid word picture of a stronghold equally applicable to Blarney:

> They were a people accustomed to bestow wines, and tender beef and holiday dresses! They were graceful and beneficent; their strongholds were filled with beautiful women, and quick-slaying cavalry viewing them; mirth, playing on harps, poems and songs were at their feasts; their women were prolific, and accomplished; silken, chaste, white were the slender bodies, and sedate the eyes of their maidens! [. . .] Hilarity, drunkenness (occasional) were at their festivals! Loud sounded the song of the bards! Louder the shouting and the roar of cripples and large-bodied vagrant flatterers contending; and of soothsayers and gamblers in mutual discord. (Mac Carthy Glas, 1880, p. 70)

The 'high table' of the chieftain was probably situated against the west wall of the chamber, so that he could face the entrances in the south-east corner. Niches were provided for plate and other valuables in the western corners of the chamber. It is probable that these halls imitated in stone the layout of the timber houses used by the *derbfine,* but no examples of such buildings survive. At Blarney wall fireplaces were provided later by the enormously laborious method of quarrying the flues up through the thickness of the wall.

Although battlements were provided, the defensive features of the early tower houses were simple and not designed to withstand siege or impress the onlooker. Their sole purpose was to protect the immediate families of the *derbfine* members from assault and robbery, and to prevent a few head of cattle in the vicinity from being driven away by raiders. They were built in earlier settlements without regard for strategic strength. Often the first act in a rebellion was the 'breaking' of the clan's main castle to prevent the English from using it. The chieftains would then migrate to their fastnesses to sit out the trouble, rather than stay to defend their tower houses.

The tower houses were made more elaborate at the end of the sixteenth century with the addition of bartizans, machicolations and other features designed to impress. It was only during the Nine Years War (1594–1603) that Irish chieftains were forced by circumstance to convert tower houses into strategic forts; a use for which most were deeply unsuited, given that their sites had usually been dictated by social and agricultural considerations. These late tower houses show the influence of gunnery in their design, and some even incorporate trapezoidal bastions at their corners. Mashanaglas was the castle of the hereditary Mac Sweeney mercenaries of the Muskerry lords, and compared with Blarney it is a masterpiece of military design, with gunloops placed to enfilade all the approaches. Such late tower houses were internally more complex in their social arrangement, because care was taken to segregate the chieftain's family and high-status entourage from the *Ceithearn Tighe* (the complement of household guards).

By the mid sixteenth century tower houses relied increasingly on defences with a circuit of walls and conventional military features. It therefore became practical to move domestic functions such as bakehouses and kitchens out of the tower itself and into other more modern buildings within the external walls. The open court that can be seen at Kilcrea was entered from the north and is nearly intact (Butler 1910, p. 175: plan). Parapets along the north and south walls and a defensive tower show that the enclosure was defensive rather than domestic.

There is plenty of evidence for the addition of more comfortable domestic wings in tower houses in the seventeenth century (Leask 1964, p. 133). A 'new house of stone' certainly existed at Blarney by 1654 (MacCarthy 1990, p. 162) which was very probably incorporated into the eighteenth-century house. These buildings also included additional defences to the entrance in the design. A late-seventeenth-century timber stair for this purpose survives at Castle Salem (De Breffny and Ffolliot 1975, p. 75). The domestic wing at Castle Salem may have originated as an open court of the sort that survives at Kilcrea.

It is now generally accepted that most tower houses were surrounded by clusters of buildings (Jordan, 1991, p. 137). *Badhún*, cow enclosures also called bawns, stood within these ephemeral settlements. The term's exclusive association with tower houses is a modern usage (Nicholls 1993a, p. 405). The Irish may have referred to the tower houses themselves as '*daingen*', as in the phrase used when Ua Ruairc of Brefnei put his 'flocks and herds into a keep' – '*do cur a caeraidheacht a n-daingen*' (Lucas 1989, p. 118).

The tower house may be thought of as the 'hard centre' of a 'soft settlement' (Neill 1983, p. 81) whose bawns provided defence against wolves (Ó Danachair 1979, p. 158) and thieves but not much else. In some cases tower houses and bawns were built simultaneously, elsewhere the tower house could be a stand-alone structure with other adjacent structures built later. The bawns, however, were critical to the operation of the strongholds as a centre of subsistence. Most towerhouse sites were further developed in various ways and these subsidiary buildings took many forms. At Blarney the tower house was surrounded by enclosures, walls and bastions covering several hectares. Parts of these survive, but a coherent plan cannot be perceived at present.

Where evidence survives, the evolution of these enclosures shows little strategic thought. Some tower houses had 'topographically dictated' irregular enclosures around their bases which fall into no clear category: an example was excavated and destroyed at Castle Inch, not far from Blarney, in advance of the construction of a hydro-electric scheme (Fahy 1957, Fig. 1). Typically compounds were attached to different faces of the tower as required. The tower house guarded the bawn, which might be entered through a gatehouse next to the tower house. The angles of the bawn were often defended by turrets or bastions with gunloops.

Kitchens were often built outside the tower and can sometimes be identified by their vaulted bread ovens. Additional ground-floor halls were provided for hospitality. We know from documentary sources that several tower houses in West Cork had external halls. The ground-floor hall, stone, clay or timber, was probably a constant feature of the *derbfine* stronghold. Stanyhurst in *De Rebus in Hibernia* stated that castles were (in translation)

> united, by a close connexion, [with] fairly large and spacious halls, constructed of a compound of potter's earth and mud. These are not securely roofed either with quarried slates, or with rough hewn stones or tiles, but are as a rule thatched with straw from the fields. In these halls they usually take their meals; they seldom however sleep except in the castles because it is possible for their enemies with great ease to apply to the covering of the halls blazing torches. (Leask 1951, p. 124)

The term 'a close connexion' accurately describes the relationship of the two structures, neither being subordinate to the other. These ephemeral timber and clay halls were probably universal features next to the fifteenth-century tower houses. Later tower houses, with their more sophisticated designs, seem not to have needed them. As in French seigneurial architecture (Jones et al. 1989, p. 87), a suite of 'high-' and 'low-status halls' was provided within the tower house itself. Blarney shows adaptation from the early 'single-hall' form to a socially segregated 'multiple-hall' form.

Given that a tower house was something of a status symbol, the question arises how the building of a tower house was paid for. The Gaelic economy was essentially coinless until the sixteenth century; coinage was known and used but it was not central to the system of exchange (Simms 1987, p. 148).

There is documentary evidence that in Tipperary, among the various branches of the Butlers, castle construction was carried out by forced labour, which was imposed on people in their territory (Neill 1984, p. 79). The Earl of Desmond is known to have imposed the *musteron* (a tax for masons) to pay for repairs to castles, bridges and other 'public works' (Donnelly 1994, p. 78).

There is no evidence of such direct impositions by his rival, the Lord of Muskerry, for castle building, but in the fifteenth century some of the labour and materials required for tower-house construction were probably exacted from the population at large, following the custom of 'coign and livery'. Exactions could be used to force ordinary clan members to repair or construct buildings (Ellis 1985, p. 41). If muscle power was supplied by coercion of landless labourers, the construction of a tower house could be a largely cash-free enterprise, but a chieftain who drove his 'churls' too hard ran the risk that they would move away from his land and he would lose their labour (Samuel 1998, p. 47). It must be inferred that a largely professional workforce had to be hired if the work was to be carried out quickly. Some cash would probably have been needed for the employment of a few key craftsmen, who seem to have recorded their work on tally-sticks (Bennett 1869, pp. 193–4).

A legend recounts how the later Ballynacarriga Castle was built for free: the chieftain entertained his masons royally while they worked for him, but when they presented their tally-sticks he drove them off with threats (ibid.). This method of payment survived in the Dunmanway area into the twentieth century (Gibbings 1952, p. 57).

There were other forms of payment apart from hospitality and cash. In Fermanagh some craftsmen were sufficiently important for their deaths to be recorded in the *Annals of Ulster* (Nicholls 1993a, p. 417) and a wright (or carpenter) attained the professional status of *ollamh* for the whole county (ibid., p. 418). It is possible that such *ollamhnachts* (official titles) were given to the fifteenth-century masons of tower houses; these included endowments of land (Simms 1987, p. 176).

Could Blarney therefore have been built without the need for money to change hands? Forced labour could not provide the necessary skills and it must be assumed that each mason had a retinue of craftsmen such as banker masons and wallers; quarrymen would also have been needed, as well as carpenters. Iron, clothes, rope, lime, withies and other materials each indicate the existence of a separate craft. The construction of a single tower house must have kept dozens of craftsmen in employment for years. Building has considerable social and economic implications because income must have been assured to keep projects going (McNeill 1985–6, p. 61).

J.A. Jordan comments that there is a 'relationship between size of tower houses and the quality of land' (1991, p. xii) but it is perhaps more accurate to see this as an indirect correlation. The size of a tower house seems to bear a stronger correlation to the status of the family who built it. The Mac Carthy Muskerry were in constant rivalry with the Fitzgerald Earls of Desmond for the overlordship of Munster (O'Brien 1993, p. 139) and it is hardly surprising that the Muskerry tower houses were large and few, reflecting the exceptional levels of central control exerted by this clan. This phenomenon has also been observed in Limerick (Donnelly 1994, p. 139). Enclosure castles of Norman origin were frequently re-employed (McNeill 1997, p. 206). Castlemore, a neglected enclosure castle first built by the Anglo-Norman Cogans, was later taken by the Mac Carthy Muskerry. When a 'greenfield' site was available, the clan opted for a 'super tower house', such as Kilcrea.

CHAPTER 4

The Mac Carthy Muskerry

In 1824 Crofton Croker wrote the following:

> It would be a matter of little importance and considerable labour to trace the Castle
> of Blarney from one possessor to another [. . .] but a tiresome repetition of names,
> occasioned by the scantness of them in an exceedingly numerous family, present
> continual problems of perplexity to the general reader. (pp. 292–3)

The history of the Mac Carthy Muskerry family is indeed sometimes difficult to unravel because the male members of the *derbfine* restricted themselves to a very limited choice of personal names (Cormac was the favourite). A bewildering variety of variants were used. Historians therefore refer to the chieftains by number, for exmple 'the eleventh lord'. These are shown in the three genealogical tables (Figs. 3, 4 and 5).

It may be helpful for the reader to bear in mind the following rules: a Muskerry male *derbfine* member would be called, say, Dermot mhic (Mac) Teige (son of Teige). If he had the same name as his father, he would be called Dermot Óg (Oge) or 'young Dermot' to distinguish him. This name might follow him into old age. His full name would also include the clan and sept 'tag', if appropriate, which originated as a nickname of the sept founder, e.g., Fínghin Mac Carthy Riabhach (swarthy). A chieftain would on succession be called '*the* Mac Carthy Mor' or '*the* O'Rahilly', being the personification of the clan. There was a feminine version for women's names, e.g., Ellen ni Cormac (Ellen, daughter of Cormac). Noblewomens' names were much more diverse, in part because of the custom of marrying outside the clan.

The Mac Carthy family had always lived as a single clan since, it is alleged, pagan times. The land on which they built Blarney Castle had not always been theirs, but they had had interests in the area before written records were kept. In the twelfth century, when Muskerry's written history commenced, it formed part of the kingdom of Cork, then ruled by Dermot Mac Carthy of Desmond (Otway-Ruthven 1993, p. 49). The title 'king' in this case meant 'overlord' and he was not the direct ruler of Co. Cork. He seems to have been based at Shandon, near Cork City. Desmond was a large and powerful territory, which later included lands in most of the counties of Munster.

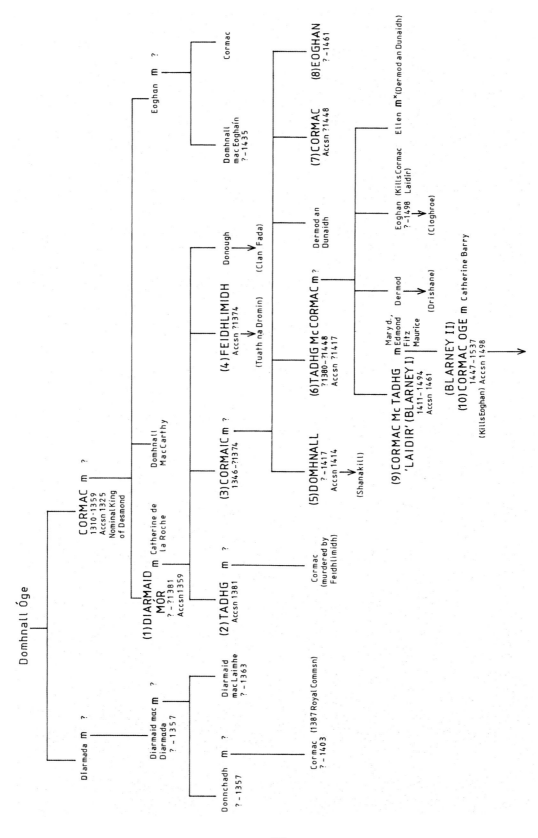

Fig. 3 Genealogical table: the origin of the Muskerry lordship.

In the second half of the twelfth century Cork, like other parts of Ireland, was subject to a series of incursions by land-hungry Welsh-Norman families. The Norman invasion was a piecemeal business. These adventurers were usually from South Wales. They took small pockets of land at first, and gradually expanded their holdings either through marriages or other alliances with the Irish chieftains. In this way the English king Henry II (1154–89) gained control of further territory at very little cost to the Crown. He generously made huge grants of lands to Norman families despite the fact that this land was still in Irish hands. Although the Mac Carthy King of Cork had sworn fealty to the English Crown, Henry nevertheless granted most of the Mac Carthy territory to Miles de Cogan and Robert Fitz Stephen after 1177 (ibid., p. 61). During the thirteenth century another Anglo-Norman family, the Fitzgeralds, otherwise known as the Geraldines, took Desmond from the Mac Carthys bit by bit. This family in due course became the Earls of Desmond, powerful and unfriendly neighbours to Muskerry.

The Mac Carthys began to regain territory in Cork, particularly after the battle of Callan in 1261, when one Fineen Mac Carthy inflicted heavy losses on the Normans. The Desmonds were also defeated in Co. Kerry and a centuries-long enmity between the Desmonds and the Mac Carthys was established.

After the battle of Callan it was said that 'no Desmond durst put plough in ground for twelve years in his own country' (Gillman 1892a, p. 18). Instability and under-investment also paved the way for the resurgence of Gaelic power. Written sources on the period are rare, but one annal tells that in 1280 the nominal king of Desmond, Domhnal Ruadh, divided up the territories remaining under his rule. He gave the areas north of the Lee to Feidhlimdh Mac Carthy, and those to the south to Domhnal Og Maol, whose successors gradually forced the Anglo-Normans eastwards out of West Cork (Nicholls 1993b, p. 165).

In 1300 the lands between the Rivers Blackwater and Lee were still held by the de Cogans. This was where Blarney Castle would be built and would form the heartlands of Mac Carthy Muskerry power (Fig. 1). The de Cogans' centre of power was at Castlemore, whose ivy-covered and neglected ruins are well worth visiting. Their lands extended from the west shores of Cork harbour to the fertile Bride Valley. However, in the following decades a number of the de Cogan heirs died young, in battle or otherwise, and the leadership of the family repeatedly fell to children. Divided inheritances and marriage portions also reduced their power and territory before the final blow fell.

During the thirteenth and fourteenth centuries the Mac Carthy clan divided into three major families or septs. The largest grouping was that of the Mac Carthy Mór ('great'). The second was the Mac Carthy Riabhach (Anglicised 'Reagh'; 'swarthy'), a clan dominant in Carbery (Fig. 2); its first 'prince' was recognised in 1366 (Gillman 1892a, p. 17). The last, and wealthiest, was the Mac Carthy Muskerry, who came to rule that territory. The first lord of Muskerry, Dermot Mac Cormac, acceded in 1359, a century before the building of Blarney Castle.

Little is known of the lives and activities of the early chieftains of the sept. The monastic histories (annals) tend to record their victories in battle or their deaths, also usually in battle. The details of day-to-day life are lost. The motivation behind recorded actions can usually be only guessed at. The events that do come into view give a disproportionately warlike image of the clan, and it must be remembered that their wealth and influence was due to long settled peaceful periods rather than frequent bouts of fighting.

The death of the head of the de Cogan lineage in 1330 meant that the control of the family again fell to a minor. The Black Death (bubonic plague) arrived in Ireland in 1348, hitting the towns and Lordship of Ireland much more severely than the lightly populated Gaelic areas. More than half the population of Cork City is reputed to have died by 1351 (Otway-Ruthven 1993, p. 268). The plague remained endemic in Ireland, with outbreaks recurring into the sixteenth century. By 1348 the plague probably dealt the de Cogans their death blow, making defence of their borders hopeless. Dermod Mor Mac Carthy, (Diamuid mac Diarmaida) of Duhallow, the nemesis of the de Cogans, was born in 1310, and by this time he was over-running the de Cogan lands. In the long run neither he nor his sons benefited from their success, but this was the beginning of Mac Carthy domination of Muskerry.

Although Co. Cork was now ruled according to Gaelic custom, it still had the technical status of an English shire, which meant that the English Crown appointed justices to try criminal pleas throughout the county. The area under these assizes declined steadily throughout the fourteenth century with the Gaelic reinvasion, and by the fifteenth century only the port towns retained a tenuous link with the English administration and few or no representatives were sent to Parliament (Nicholls 1993b, p. 162). The Anglo-Norman office of *shire-reeve* (sheriff) temporarily sank into oblivion, having degenerated into an honorific title held by lords in the north and east of the county with no effective jurisdiction.

The English did not accept Mac Carthy rule in Cork without a fight. A new *justiciar* of Ireland was appointed, Sir Thomas de Rokeby. In addition to carrying out a general overhaul of the Irish administration (Otway-Ruthven 1993, p. 268), he turned his attention to the troubles in the south-west of the country. In 1352 he moved the government to Cork City, which he used as a base from which to expel Dermod Mor Mac Carthy from the de Cogan lands. Nevertheless, the de Cogans were so unwilling to return to their lands that de Rokeby went to the lengths of telling them that it would be forfeit (taken) if they did not take possession again. After their expulsion from the de Cogan lands, the Duhallow Mac Carthys (Dermot Mor and his son Donnchadh Mac Dermot) died in a feud with some O'Sullivans at Duhallow in 1356–7 and some of the de Cogans began to venture back after this.

It seems that after this date the Duhallow (Mac Donogh) and Muskerry families became geographically distinct. Cormac Mac Carthy, the 'nominal king of Desmond', a cousin of the Duhallow Mac Carthys, was chieftain of the Mac Carthy Muskerry. He seems to have independently helped de Rokeby (ibid., p. 279). He was subsequently granted many of the old de Cogan lands, including Macroom, and thus profited by his relative's rebellion, but he died in 1359. De Rokeby also helped himself and his heirs to lands in Muskerry at the expense of the hapless Walter de Cogan, the last representative of the lineage.

Cormac Mac Carthy's predecessors had annexed West Muskerry long before the lordship was created. They achieved this by importing a clan of mercenaries, the MacSweeneys, from Donegal, who were then allowed to settle in much of West Muskerry in exchange for their services. The MacSweeneys remained the trusted guardians of Muskerry for over three hundred years (McCarthy 1922, p. 177).

Cormac Mac Carthy's son Dermod Mor was considered to be the first Lord of Muskerry by 1359, having allegedly been given this title by the English in 1353 (ibid.), but there seems to be some confusion about this. He also married into an Anglo-Norman family; his wife was Catherine de la Roche.

The English Crown was aware that affairs in Ireland were slipping out of its control. In spring 1361, during a lull in the course of the Hundred Years War between France and England, Edward III turned his attention to the deteriorating situation in Ireland (Otway-Ruthven 1993, p. 285). He sent his son Lionel, Duke of Clarence, to Ireland with a great army. Much of Clarence's time was spent dealing with arguments between his young cronies and the Anglo-Irish or improving the facilities of Dublin Castle for his wife. His sojourn in Ireland is, however, famous for the drafting of the 'Statutes of Kilkenny', which in essence sought to outlaw Gaelic culture with particular emphasis on preventing the Anglo-Irish from becoming 'more Irish than the Irish themselves'.

It appears that Clarence came south with his army in 1365 and campaigned throughout Muskerry (ibid., p. 294), though nothing much is known about this. Land which had been 'wasted' by the Irish was granted to the Barrets and the Mac Carthys. This included the old de Cogan lands in Muscrimittine, which seem to have been regarded as vacant. A now-lost grant of lands to Domhnall, the elder son of Cormac Mac Carthy, in 1365 may have included part of Muskerry. This was presumably in gratitude for Mac Carthy support of de Rokeby or perhaps in realpolitik recognition that Cormac's sons were the strongest local force. Domhnall's younger brothers, Diarmuid and Eoghan, were certainly the long-term beneficiaries of this grant. Dermot Mór, who was given the tag Muscraighe (Muskerry) was the first lord of Muskerry. He died in 1381 at the hands of the O'Mahonys 'in treachery', probably because he wanted their lands south of the Lee. The three septs of the O'Mahonys were allowed to stay put (Fig. 2) subject to a small 'head rent' until the general confiscation of Gaelic lands by Cromwell in 1642 (McCarthy 1922, p. 177).

After the departure of Clarence, royal authority continued to shrink inexorably. For the next twenty years *justiciars* good and bad dealt with repeated Gaelic incursions, but were unable to achieve much. The absence of a professional army was compounded by the failure of the feudal system. Anglo-Norman magnates were not prepared to help the Crown unless they themselves were under attack. As a result, the Lordship of Ireland became increasingly preoccupied with the defence of the eastern territories that remained under its control.

The second to eighth lords of Muskerry are shadowy figures who lived and died before the construction of Blarney Castle. Even their dates of birth, accession and death are uncertain (Fig. 3). Fitful gleams of light are cast by royal records, which indicate that even at this early date attempts were being made to get the Mac Carthy lord to act as a loyal subject. According to a pedigree preserved at Lambeth Palace, Dermod Mor was succeeded first by his son Tadhg (second Lord). Tadhg was appointed by Richard II to membership of a royal commission of the peace for Co. Cork, together with a Duhallow Mac Carthy. The Crown may have made these surprising appointments in an attempt to balance these Irish lords against the Anglo-Norman families in Cork, whose loyalty was questionable at the best of times. A tradition of cooperation between the Muskerry lords and the Crown may date from this time.

Tadhg was succeeded by his brothers Cormac (third Lord) and Feidhlimidh (fourth Lord). Feidhlimidh murdered his nephew Cormac Mac Tadhg. This lineage killing should have disqualified him and his descendants from the chieftainship (ibid., p. 178). However, he continued as chieftain until after 1411 (Nicholls 1993b, p. 172).

The succession after this is somewhat murky, it seems possible that Muskerry was effectively divided between two branches of the family. Feidhlimidh was succeeded by his nephew Dohmnall Mac Cormac (fifth Lord). His short period as chieftain ended in 1417 and he was succeeded by Tadhg Mac Cormac (sixth Lord), his brother, a very long-lived chieftain, who died in 1461. During this period it appears that part of the territory fell under the control of Feidhlimidh's cousins Cormac and Domhnall, sons of Eoghan the son of Dermot Mor.

Cormac and Dohmnall were grandsons of Cormac, the nominal prince of Desmond. Although they never became chieftains, they carried out further expansion of the territory at the expense of the Barrets, whom they defeated in 1421, as well as the Mac Carthy Reaghs and the Roche family (ibid., p. 173). This suggests that they must have attracted a following amongst part of the clan. Their success may have been the reason for conflict between the two branches of the family; Dohmnall was killed by Tadhg in 1435. The enlarged Muskerry was eventually inherited by Tadhg's eldest surviving son, Cormac MacTadhg Laidir ('the strong', 9th lord). Before him, Tadhg's two brothers Cormac Mac Cormac (7th lord) and Eoghan Mac Cormac (8th lord) held the chieftainship in succession. Perhaps Tadhg's lineage killing of his cousin Dohmnall Mac Eoghan was not considered sufficiently important to prevent his son Cormac becoming chieftain. It was Cormac who is traditionally believed to have built Blarney.

At this stage the Mac Carthys did not rule all of Muskerry; parts of it had recently been won from the Barrets but some O'Mahony septs still held lands there. It is not clear when the Mac Carthys imposed their overlordship on these O'Mahonys, but the territory where Kilcrea castle and Friary were built had been part of the O'Mahony territory of Kinalmeaky, held under the overlordship of the Mac Carthy Reagh, until quite recently. When Cormac Laidir became Lord of Muskerry the land Blarney was built on was still in the hands of the Anglo-Norman Lombard family.

The Mac Carthy Muskerry castles

The Mac Carthy Muskerry had a number of tower houses in their territory. These eventually included Blarney, Castle Inch, Carrignamuck, Kilcrea, Cloghphilip, Ballea, Macroom and

Cloghroe (Fig. 1). Blarney was the most important castle for much of its history and probably became the chieftain's seat after Cormac Laidir's chieftainship. The chief members of the *derbfine* occupied certain lands according to status or seniority, which were redistributed on the death of the chieftain (Ch. 2). This regular redistribution was later formalised by the building of tower houses on these lands, and the presence of these strongholds would have encouraged a stable succession. Other tower houses in the territory belonged to the various professional families in the service of the clan, but they had to be open to the chieftain and his wife at all hours.

The tanist was usually housed in Carrignamuck (Gillman 1892a, p. 18) or Castle Inch and moved to Blarney when he became chieftain. This was not a hard and fast rule: one chieftain chose to remain at Castle Inch throughout his life (Ó Murchadha 1985, p. 16). Cormac Laidir was reputed to be the builder of Carrignamuck Castle (Fig. 2), third in size after Blarney and Kilcrea.

There is a legendary assertion that the site of Blarney was occupied by a timber hunting 'box' (lodge) of Dermot Mac Carthy Mor, King of Desmond, which was rebuilt in 1200 (McCarthy 1922, p. 179). It is not impossible that such a site was inhabited by the Mac Carthys prior to the Anglo-Norman invasion but no structure we now see is earlier than the final decades of the fifteenth century (Sweetman 1999, p. 163). Any romantic legend of occupation of the site by Mac Carthys 'time out of mind' is punctured by documentary evidence (see below). About the only certainty is that Blarney Castle was not all built at once, a point that has been generally accepted since a local man, C. Crawford Woods, described the castle perceptively in 1896.

The earliest form of the stronghold can be seen in the north-west tower, which formed part of a larger circuit of defences, including a north curtain wall (Crawford Woods 1896, p. 340) and at least one other tower. Although it has recently been suggested otherwise (Sweetman 1999, p. 161), the design of the north-west tower demonstrates that there was no intention to incorporate it into a larger building and this was only achieved with some difficulty (see Ch. 11).

The historical accounts do not *name* Cormac Laidir as the builder of Blarney, but he is traditionally recorded as the builder of the Observant Franciscan Friary of Kilcrea in 1465 (Nicholls 1993b, p. 173), where he was subsequently buried. The Gaelic chronicle, *The Annals of the Four Masters*, confirm that he built the friary (McCarthy 1922, p. 179). Kilcrea Friary is a well-preserved National Monument and was used as the clan mausoleum for centuries. Cormac Laidir is also traditionally credited with the building of a tower house near the friary (Gillman 1892a, p. 18). The grouping of friary and castle may indicate a plan to create a more permanent settlement or even a town on the Anglo-Norman model.

A fondness for the gentle, fertile landscape of the Bride Valley would explain the building of this very large and magnificent tower. Kilcrea Castle was provided with gunloops (Samuel 1998, p. 628) and the introduction of guns to Ireland can be dated quite closely to 1487 (Simms 1975, p. 108). This would place the start of construction at Kilcrea Castle, on present evidence, near the very end of Cormac's chieftainship in 1494. It seems more likely to have begun under his successor, Cormac Oge. The similarities in detail of Kilcrea and Blarney indicate that Kilcrea and the secondary part of Blarney are contemporary. Nevertheless, given his proclivity for building (he also built another religious house at Ballymacadane, near Cork City), it is natural to wonder whether Cormac Laidir was the builder of Blarney Castle.

A vanished inscription on the south wall of the oldest part of the building is supposed to have read '*Cormach Mac Carthy Fortis Mi Fieri Fecit* (had me built) AD *1446*' (Black 1857, p. 151); this stone can no longer be identified. This attribution to Cormac Laidir could be a fabrication by the family in later years: such date stones are extremely unusual before about 1570. In reality the family's claim to the site was relatively recent and this stone may have been intended to link Blarney to a more illustrious past and progenitor than was the case. Cormac Laidir was not actually chieftain in 1446.

In 1488 Eoghan, Cormac's brother, gained the lands of Cloghroe and Cloghphilip in the neighbourhood of Blarney. As a leading *derbfine* member he could act with considerable autonomy, and in 1479 he may also have used force to acquire the valley of Blarney, which belonged to the Anglo-Norman Lombard family. It has therefore been suggested by Kenneth Nicholls that Blarney was more probably built in the 1480s (1993b, p. 173). This would make the earlier part Eoghan's work rather than his brother's.

A sixteenth-century dispute about the ownership of Blarney throws further light on its origins. Blarney had formed part of an Anglo-Norman manor called Gynes or Cloghroe. The whole manor had belonged to the Crown but had been granted to one Lombard, the Constable of Cloghroe Castle, in the time of Edward III (Collins 1954, pp. 2–3). The Lombards held it until at least 1479, when it is mentioned in the will of David Lombard (Nicholls 1993, p. 173). The Mac Carthys seem to have gained it from the Lombard family during the 1480s, probably by force of arms, as claimed in a late sixteenth-century legal case (Ch. 6; Collins 1954, p. 2).

Acquisition of the valleys of Blarney and Cloghroe drove a bridge of Mac Carthy territory through the lands of their rivals and created a common border with the influential Earls of Desmond (Fig. 2).

The chieftainship of Cormac Laidir

As well as building religious houses Cormac Laidir was renowned for enforcing the observance of the Sabbath throughout his lands, but like that of any healthy chieftain, his rule was not entirely devoted to architecture and religion. He assisted the young Earl of Desmond during a struggle for the Desmond Earldom in 1468 to 1470. In 1477 he was allegedly responsible for throwing the southern half of Munster into turmoil when he took the Mac Carthy Reagh chieftain prisoner in a foray, assisted by his cousins, the sons of Dermod an Dunaidh.

The English Crown was weakened at this time because of the civil war known as the Wars of the Roses in England. Edward IV was forced to rely on the Desmonds, who carried on the war in Ireland on behalf of the Yorkists, defeating forces loyal to the Lancastrians in 1462. This was the height of Desmond power, but six years later the Earl was beheaded by the Crown in mysterious circumstances. After this date the Desmonds became disaffected opponents of royal power. A long succession struggle followed which greatly weakened the Earl's power over his tenants and clients (Ellis 1985, p. 55). The estrangement of successive Desmond earls from the Crown ensured that English influence in Munster was greatly reduced. Desmond's decline provided an opportunity for the Mac Carthy Muskerry, and the Crown increasingly relied on him as a counter to Desmond power in Cork.

Cormac was able to force the English settlers of Muskerry to pay him a 'blackrent', a form of protection money, of 40 pounds a year to stop his henchmen from persecuting them (Gillman 1892a, p. 18). He continued to expand his lands north-eastwards into the Barret and Roche territories when he secured a commandery of the Knights Hospitallers (an order of knights that originated in the Holy Land) at Mourne Abbey near Mallow. As an Irish lord he was also able to demand 'rectorial tithes' from churches; this was one of the many peculiarities of the Gaelic Church, over which the Pope exercised only tenuous control. Ironically it was Tudor attempts to impose Protestantism on Ireland that made it a stronghold of Catholic conformism.

The accession of Henry Tudor to the English throne in 1485 as Henry VII brought an end to the Wars of the Roses, but during his reign he had to fight off challenges from two young pretenders to the throne, Lambert Simnel and Perkin Warbeck. Both aroused considerable sympathy and support in Ireland, where Simnel managed to raise an army. Evidently Cormac Laidir remained loyal to the Crown during this excitement, since shortly after this Henry VII granted him a charter of English liberty (Ellis 1985, p. 70) in 1488. The second pretender, Perkin Warbeck, claimed to be Richard, Duke of York, Edward IV's second son. He landed at Cork City in November 1491. Again, Cormac Laidir seems to have avoided getting involved although Warbeck received widespread support in Munster before Henry VII's allies frustrated his plans. He departed in 1492 for the French court (ibid., p. 72). Desmond's support for Perkin Warbeck resulted in fines rather than execution; other rebels were not so lucky and royal control over the area was strengthened.

In 1494 Cormac's chieftainship ended when he was wounded by his brother Eoghan and his nephews in a fracas at Carriganamuck Castle. He died of his wounds and was buried at his new friary at Kilcrea. Eoghan was accepted as chieftain, regardless of the lineage killing; however, he is not included in the numbered sequence of chieftains, which reflects his questionable status. Eoghan Mac Tadhg ruled from 1495 to 1498, before he died at the hand of Cormac Laidir's son Cormac Oge, who then ruled as tenth Lord, from 1498 to 1537. Cormac Oge inherited his father's longevity as well as his position and was still actively ruling at the age of 90. Father and son made the Mac Carthys the most powerful and wealthy Gaelic clan in Cork. As the historian Kenneth Nicholls has said, 'the powerful and grasping Mac Carthys of Muskerry seem to have exercised a degree of control within their territory rare for Gaelic rulers' (1993b, p. 158).

CHAPTER 5

Muskerry in the First Half of the Sixteenth Century

B Y 1500 THE MAC CARTHY Muskerry territorial expansion was essentially complete, and while subsequent additions were made, the enduring foundations of MacCarthy power in East Muskerry, with its constellation of *derbfine* castles, had been laid. The eastern expansion of Mac Carthy Muskerry lands was a haphazard process that created an extremely fragmented border (Nicholls 1993b, p. 173); elsewhere the borders followed hills and rivers in a more logical manner. It is from this date that Blarney became the centre of Mac Carthy Muskerry operations as they played their role in the convulsions of the Tudor reconquest of Ireland. The map of Muskerry in 1600 (Fig. 1) is based on a map that shows the main castles and settlements around Blarney and was made by the English (Ó Murchadha 1985, p. xii). It is possible to plot these on a modern map to give a skeletal idea of the main concentrations of population (Fig. 2).

Since the Mac Carthy Muskerry chieftain traced his descent from the former royal line of Desmond, he recognised no overlord (Nicholls 1993b, p. 158), except, when convenient, the Crown. The authority of the English Crown in this area was largely token outside the sea ports until the introduction of the Council of Munster in 1569, leaving the Mac Carthy Muskerry considerable autonomy. Despite this, hollow claims to surrounding lands were made by important lords as a matter of course. In the 1580s, for example, Mac Carthy Mor tried to revive long extinct exactions from the Mac Carthy Muskerry and Mac Carthy Duhallow. Although the Mac Carthys, between them, held sway over much of West Cork, it was further broken up into a bewildering mass of fractions (Fig. 1), and the area along the coast shows how new septs of ancient clans from elsewhere in Ireland would move into an area as the vassals of the Mac Carthy Reagh. These septs displaced older native clans to the west and grew into strong clans in their own right, but it was not forgotten that the Mac Carthy Reagh was their overlord. The Lord President of Munster, Sir George Carew, wrote (in 1599) that

> O'Mahon's country doeth follow the ancient tanist law of Ireland; and unto whom MacCarthy [Reagh] shall give a white rod, he is O'Mahon, or lord of the country; but the giving of the rod avails nothing except that he be chosen by the followers, not yet the election without the rod. (MacCarthy Glas 1867, p. 12)

In exactly the same way the subservient Healy clan were usually followers of the Mac Carthy Muskerry, their chieftains had to pay him a fee of £4 9s on being inaugurated.

Henry VIII ascended to the English throne in 1509. He never visited Ireland but his political and religious policies were to have a lasting impact on the country. Although he treated English rebels and Irish enemies as the same class of 'disobeisant subjects' (Ellis 1985, p. 112), he was forced by a lack of finance to adopt a gradualist and conciliatory policy in Ireland.

Henry wanted the Irish to give up their distinctive customs and laws in exchange for recognition as landholders under his rule. His canny father, Henry VII, had been working along very similar lines, and it had seemed a natural step to make a personal grant of 'English liberty' to Cormac Laidir (ninth Lord) in 1488 (see above). The grant held out the possibility that Cormac Laidir would eventually be rewarded with charters for his lands (ibid.). Here, a stumbling block emerges; such a grant was an absurdity in Irish law because the Muskerry clanlands did not belong to the chieftain and never could, since they were the property of the clan as a whole. Despite this, the concept of 'surrender and regrant' was developed into a major policy in the 1540s and played an important role later, in the reign of Elizabeth I. Individual chieftains learnt to operate the two opposing systems in tandem, acting as a landlord in dealings with the Crown and its administration while also being a traditional chieftain to their people.

The governance of Ireland under Henry VIII was largely left to the Earl of Kildare, and Ireland fell into complete disorder with his connivance. In 1520 the Earl of Surrey was dispatched from England as Lord Lieutenant to save the situation with what amounted to a small peace-keeping force. With difficulty he restored the status quo in those areas normally under the control of the Crown. He wrote that he was wasting his own time and health, as well as the king's money, unless realistic funding was committed to the task (ibid., p. 114). Surrey spelt out the resources that would be required in a detailed plan of invasion. Henry responded that the Irish could be made into loyal subjects through 'sober ways, politic shifts and amiable persuasion' (ibid., p. 111). The Mac Carthy Muskerry chieftain, Cormac Oge (tenth Lord), was seen as a model Gaelic noble, on whom high hopes were pinned.

Despite Surrey's mission, in 1521 the Desmonds exploited the situation to attack their old enemies, the Mac Carthys. James, the head of the Fitzgeralds, overran Munster with an army of cavalry and Cormac Oge called a 'rising out' of the clan, joined by the forces of his son-in-law Cormac Mac Carthy Reagh. Together they nearly annihilated the male lineage of the Desmonds at the battle of Mourne Abbey. Surrey wrote to Henry VIII that Desmond was little loss, due to his disloyalty, while Cormac Oge was praised as an Irishman 'who would most gladly fall into English order' (Gillman 1892a, pp. 18–19).

In 1528 Cormac Oge attended the Irish Parliament as 'Lord of Muscry' (ibid., p. 19). In the same year he aided Lord James Butler and the Sheriff of Cork, Sir John Fitzgerald, in their campaign against the Desmonds (Ellis 1985, p. 117), who had joined forces with Kildare to attack the loyalist

Earl of Ormond. The indirect rule of Ireland by powerful nobles was becoming unviable.

The new Earl of Desmond wanted recognition from the Crown, and the epicentre of events shifted away from Cork. Kildare, also known as 'Silken Thomas', led a serious revolt in Dublin, the heart of the Lordship, in 1534. This revolt was encouraged and fomented, for the first time, by religious difference and the hope of international aid. After the crushing of Kildare's rebellion there was a shift away from government by local magnates in favour of men in the service of the Crown, civil servants, often clever men from humble backgrounds rather than aristocrats.

From about 1530 we benefit from a vastly increased body of documentation, mostly English-language and mostly hostile. Pardons, complaints before Parliament, depositions, inquisitions, fiants, campaign diaries and other 'official' records provide a relatively fulsome if consistently biased view of Gaelic life and institutions. The appearance of wills in the sixteenth century allows the authentic voice of Muskerry chieftains to be directly heard for the first time.

When Cormac Oge died in 1537 he was buried with his father in the Friary of Kilcrea. He was suceeded by his son Teige Mac Cormac Oge (eleventh Lord), who was 55 years old. Teige's son Dermot was installed as tanist at Carrignamuck Castle. (He too was not to succeed until he was well on in years.) In September of the same year four high-ranking English commissioners arrived in Dublin with the power to inquire into and reform all abuses in government. The gist of their reforms was that the relationship between the Crown and 'Englishry' should be reformed to follow the lines of English government. A traditional relationship would be maintained with Irish chieftains, who were required to give pledges not to breach the peace, but who would otherwise not be interfered with (Ellis 1985, p. 133). A central administration, which had only controlled the Pale (the area around Dublin), was now expected to directly administer the areas of Leinster and Munster, where royal government had been comparatively weak. Muskerry bordered this area but by choice the Mac Carthy Muskerry had tended to support the Crown, at least against the Desmonds. With no increase in funding or staff, it is no wonder that Henry hoped for a change of heart in the Irish.

After a further serious revolt and the recall and execution of the Lord Deputy Lieutenant responsible, the new Lord Deputy Lieutenant, Sir Anthony St Leger, arrived in 1540. This marked the start of a new period of effective English rule. The policy of making the major Gaelic lords part of a new fully Anglicised kingdom was pursued by defeating some and bringing others into negotiations. For the first time, each chief was bound by indenture to recognise the king as his liege lord, to apply for a crown grant of his lands and a peerage, and meanwhile to attend Parliament and resist papal jurisdiction (ibid., p. 137). Subsidiary stages of the process would convert the Gaelic lord into a conventional titled landholder through the process of 'surrender and regrant', by which he would give up his clan's territory to the Crown, and it would then be granted by the Crown to the chieftain personally. His clan members would become his tenants. Irish society would finally be organised on the basis of landlord-and-tenant relationships governed by legal agreements. This system had gradually replaced the feudal system in England since the fourteenth century and was now to replace the traditional Gaelic landholding system.

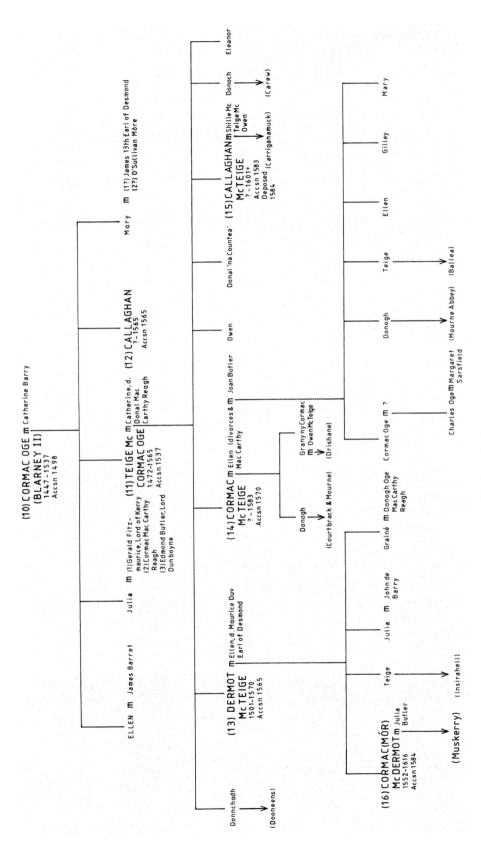

Fig. 4 Genealogical table: posterity of Cormac Oge Mac Carthy (to 1616).

St Leger's conciliatory approach included the recognition in 1541 of new Geraldine lords of Kildare and Desmond, in return for their cooperation. St Leger's right-hand man, Thomas Cusack, commented that 'the winning of the earl of Desmond was the winning of the rest of Munster with small charges' (ibid., p. 139). An indenture of submission made by Teige Mac Cormac Oge in 1542 (Gillman 1892a, p. 30) must have formed part of St Leger's triumphal and peaceable progress around Munster. Teige and seven other Cork chieftains agreed to refer all disputes to a commission of arbitration appointed for Munster rather than use their *brehon* judges. This commission was to consist of various leading mayors and protestant bishops.

The English reformation of religion had introduced a new, complicating element into the situation. Henry had made himself head of a new entity, the Church of England, after his divorce from his first wife, Catherine of Aragon. He soon went on to create the Church of Ireland to replace (so it was hoped) Catholicism in the country (Scarisbrick 1972, p. 548). While he was styled 'Lord of Ireland' he could never be head of the Church of Ireland, since the title implied that he was no more than viceroy to the Pope (ibid., p. 549). Eventually, in June 1541, he was declared King of Ireland.

By the end of Henry VIII's reign in 1547 the great Gaelic chieftains were on the brink of accepting the Lordship of Ireland and transforming themselves into feudal lords. This process, if it had been pursued skilfully after his death, might have changed the course of history. It was, however, entirely reliant on mutual goodwill and trust. This idyll ended when it became clear that there was no way of enforcing the rule of law in the Gaelic areas in the event of internal dissension or a breakdown of goodwill. Such problems may have been overcome had not international events thrust Ireland into the limelight as a battleground of the wars of the Reformation and Counter-Reformation. Henry's daughter Elizabeth was ultimately forced into the conventional military conquest of the whole island, regardless of the huge expense and losses incurred.

CHAPTER 6

Muskerry in the Reign of Elizabeth I

ELIZABETH I'S REIGN requires a whole chapter because the events in the latter half of it had a profound effect on Irish society. It was a period in which the Mac Carthy Muskerry and Blarney played an active role. (The eventful reigns of Edward VI and Mary seem to have had little impact on Muskerry.) Elizabeth was crowned Queen of an impoverished nation in 1558. The state finances had been mishandled during the reigns of her two siblings and the country was at war with both Scotland and France. Elizabeth's immediate concern was to balance the books. This ruled out doing anything other than maintaining the status quo in Ireland. However, after two years, her administration was forced to intervene against the Great O'Neill in the north of Ireland, only to give in to all his demands two years later.

Little is recorded of the 28-year reign of Teige Mac Cormac Oge (eleventh Lord), but shortly before his death in 1565 the Earl of Desmond, Maurice Duv, led a *creaght*, a cattle-rustling raid, into Muskerry. Teige's son Dermot Mac Teige led a rising out which overtook the retreating Desmonds with their prey of Mac Carthy cows. The Desmonds were routed; Maurice was taken prisoner and then killed by four horsemen to whom he had been entrusted while Dermot continued the pursuit. Maurice's daughter Ellen was Dermot's wife, but intermarriage had not diminished the ancient grudge between the Mac Carthy Muskerry and Desmond families. The fact that an important chieftain like the Earl of Desmond could find the time to pursue cattle raids is perhaps a sign of how little he was engaged with anything happening on the larger political stage. This state of affairs would change a few years later when the Desmonds rebelled once more against the English Crown.

Teige Mac Cormac Oge was buried at Kilcrea and, according to the Lambeth genealogy referred to previously, was succeeded by his brother Callaghan Mac Cormac Oge (twelfth Lord), who died almost immediately (Gillman 1892b, p. 193). Dermot Mac Teige then became thirteenth Lord.

In 1569, during Dermot Mac Teige's chieftainship, the Crown introduced provincial councils for Munster and Connaught as a means of reducing the power of the Irish magnates (MacCarthy-Morrogh 1986, p. 2). The Munster Council was used to undermine the Gaelic system of exactions and customary dues on which local magnates were reliant, and was also to resolve disputes by arbitration. The Earl of Desmond was one magnate who was gravely affected by the proposed changeover to a regular system of rents. His power and influence at the English Court was waning, as a result of his quarrel with Ormond, for which he had been imprisoned in 1567.

In 1570 Dermot died at 'his own house' of Castle Inch. His brother and tanist, Cormac Mac Teige (fourteenth Lord), succeeded him (Ó Murchadha, p. 16). Dermot's two sons, Cormac and Teige Mac Dermot, had to wait their turn for leadership. Cormac Mac Teige was bold, clever and unscrupulous; he divorced his first wife to make a more ambitious marriage and claimed in his will that she had been already married when he 'used her' (Gillman 1892b, p. 194). This act has to be put in context. Gaelic women of good family were expected to renounce their marriages if the bond impeded their husband's career (Simms 1987, p. 115). Such laudable self-abnegation could not be explained in an English-style will.

Cormac's desire to conform to the new English order saw him surrender the sept lands to Queen Elizabeth in September 1577, and in the following year he received a grant of the 'whole country of Muskrie' on 20 July (*Irish Fiants*, p. 462). This gave him full ownership of not only the traditional chieftain lands, property held only for life, but also the lands of all his relatives and vassals. Remarkably there was no protest. His family now became freeholders and perhaps appreciated this enhanced legal position. In November 1577 he oversaw the suppression of the Friary at Kilcrea and was rewarded with the lease of its site and possessions (Gillman 1892b, p. 194). The following year he conformed to the Protestant Church and attended Parliament as 'Baron of Muskerry'. Perhaps his suppression of the Friary troubled his conscience less after he converted.

Among his many honours, Cormac Mac Teige was knighted for his loyalty, and Lord Deputy Sidney praised him as 'the rarest man that was ever born of the Irish' (Gillman 1892a, p. 31). His loyalty paid off – he held the post of Sheriff of Cork several times, a position of great responsibility and trust for a 'pure' Gaelic lord. The Munster Council and President had seen that the post, which had been an irrelevant anachronism in 1500, could be revived as an important arm of governance.

While Cormac was increasing in influence his rival the Earl of Desmond was declared a traitor on 2 November 1579 and was considered to be in rebellion against the Crown. His youngest brother, Sir James Sussex Fitzgerald, led another *creaght* into Muskerry fifteen years after the rout of the last. This was soundly defeated by the rising out of Muskerry, led by Donal, the brother and tanist of Cormac Mac Teige, resulting in the death of Sir James and 150 of his men. Fitzgerald, mortally wounded, was handed over to the President of Munster, Sir Warham St Leger, who had Fitzgerald's limbs nailed to the gates of Cork after he had been hanged, drawn and quartered (Gillman 1892a, p. 32). Donal died in the fighting from a 'dart' (perhaps a crossbow bolt) in the neck. He was succeeded as tanist by another brother, Callaghan Mac Teige of Castlemore.

Cormac Mac Teige's surrender of the clanlands of Muskerry to the Crown, and their subsequent regrant to him, was evidently a burden on his conscience as his will reveals. He

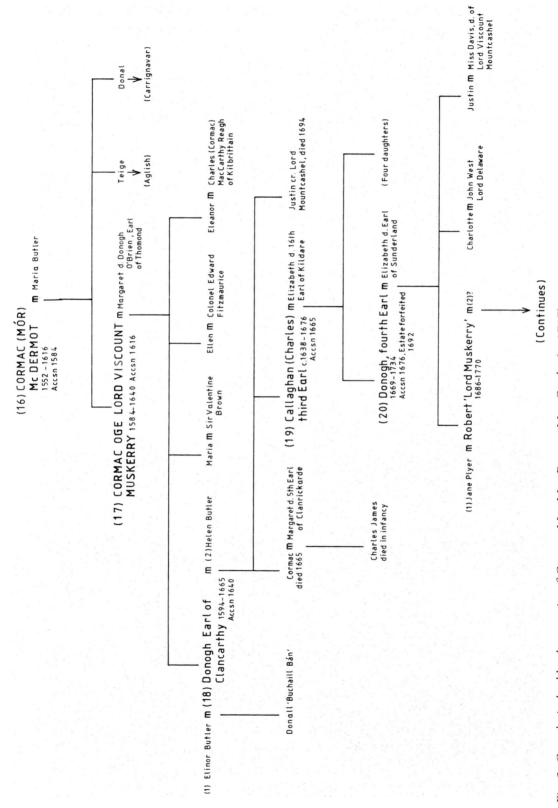

Fig. 5 Genealogical table: the posterity of Cormac Mor Mac Dermot Mac Carthy (to 1717).

succeeded in bequeathing several townlands to his younger son in 1583 (Collins 1954, p. 2) against the usual rule of reapportionment of lands, according to seniority, within the *derbfine* but his carefully laid plans for posterity were otherwise in vain. He wished to leave his new-found property to his own sons, but tradition demanded that his tanist brother, Callaghan, should have a turn as chieftain, followed by his two nephews, the sons of his other brother Dermot Mac Teige (thirteenth Lord) (Fig. 4). His will stated that his second wife, Joan Butler, was to continue to own Blarney Castle until his son was ready to be chieftain. To ensure this, he made his chief gallowglas, the warder of Blarney, one of his executors (Gillman 1892b, pp. 196–7). His intention was that his nephews Cormac and Teige Mac Dermot should never hold Blarney, even when taking turn as chieftain. They would instead continue live at their current homes, Carrignamuck and Castle Inch (ibid., p. 198).

Desmond's rebellion lasted from 1579 until his death in November 1583. Despite being restored to his lands by Elizabeth and promising to uphold various conditions, he returned to his usual habits. He was in such disfavour in England that he had little to lose from rebellion (MacCarthy-Morrogh 1986, p. 2). The Earl was eventually killed and beheaded in a glen in Co. Kerry. His lands were forfeit and from 1586 plantations were created there, bringing in a new wave of English settlers in the hope that they would accelerate the transformation of Ireland. Cultural assimilation was not to be encouraged and the adminstration had no respect for Gaelic culture.

The final decline of Desmond was a great benefit to the Mac Carthy Muskerry clan. The elimination of their most powerful neighbour and chief rival in Munster made them the most important family in the area, as well as heightening their reputation for loyalty. Instead of a single dominant neighbour their lands were now surrounded by smaller, new English settler landowners, who posed no threat to them.

The mores of the 'New English' settler culture all around them made it necessary for the Lords of Muskerry to be 'bilingual' in both speech and legal matters; as a result, we enjoy a relative wealth of surviving documentation compared with contemporary clans in areas more remote from English rule and the Common Law.

Cormac Mac Teige's death in 1583 was announced in the *Annals of the Four Masters*, a Gaelic chronicle:

> Cormac, son of Teige, son of Cormac Oge Mac Carthy, Lord of Muskerry, a comely-shaped, bright-countenanced man, who possessed most whitewashed edifices, fine-built castles, and hereditary seats of any of the descendants of Eoghan Mor, died. (McCarthy 1922, p. 192)

The entry goes on to confirm that Callaghan Mac Teige, his brother, became fifteenth Lord, only to be forced out of the chieftainship by his nephew Cormac Mac Dermot (sixteenth Lord) after only a year. Cormac Mac Dermot Mor ('great') lived through the end of Elizabeth's reign, when the Irish made common cause to expel the Lordship of Ireland with the aid of the King of Spain.

Cormac Mac Teige had intended his son Cormac Oge to eventually succeed his father as chieftain. When Cormac Mac Teige died Cormac Oge was too young to immediately contest Cormac Mac Dermot Mor's appropriations and instead he slipped away to the formidable Sir Walter Raleigh, who employed him as a page (Collins 1954, p. 2). Raleigh subsequently supported him in his long legal battle to inherit Blarney as his father had wished.

Ireland was now the focus of English interest: there was forfeited land and military glory to be gained there. Courtiers could, and did, demonstrate their military prowess against the 'wylde Iryshhe' (Cruise O'Brien 1972, illustration p. 58). This was very attractive to Queen Elizabeth, who admired military expertise, especially in handsome young men like Sir Philip Sidney. Adventurers and carpetbaggers of all ranks flocked to Ireland, gaining lands at the expense of the Gaels and the 'Old English' – long-established Norman families who were considered to have 'gone native' and who were often also considered to be too powerful and independent of the Crown.

Sir Walter Raleigh's life was bound up in the theory and practice of colonisation of the New World (MacCarthy-Morrogh 1986, p. 42). He had played an important part in the defeat of Desmond and, like an Anglo-Norman *justiciar*, he took the opportunity to obtain prime Irish lands for himself. As an undertaker in the Munster Plantation, he colonised the Desmond lands, much as he had the Roanoke colony of Virginia.

Cormac Mac Dermot Mor surrendered 'his' lands and had them regranted on 9 May 1589. This represented the ultimate expansion of the Mac Carthy Muskerry domain and included areas recently wrested from the Barrets and Roches (Nicholls 1993b, p. 174). The City of Cork was nearly encircled by a 'pincer' of Muskerry lands (Fig. 1). Cormac Oge, known as Charles McCarthy, still fighting for his inheritance, petitioned the Privy Council to get his castle and *tuath* back and argued that they did not form part of Muskerry, having been taken from the Lombard family by force of arms. His avaricious uncle therefore sought out a suitable heir of the Lombards, a Cork merchant, from whom he purchased the rights to the land (Collins 1954, p. 3). Cormac Oge subsequently claimed in an inquisition held at Cork City that a large part of the valley near Blarney at Cloghroe was long-lost Crown land, and it took some clever legal work by Cormac Mac Dermot Mor's team to have this inquisition ruled null and void in 1596. Firm title to Blarney was finally established in favour of Cormac Mac Dermot Mor. Lady Joan Butler, Cormac Oge's mother, was forced to move to the castle of Carrigadrohid.

Cormac Oge was trusted by the English authorities, but the loyalty of his self-serving cousin was questioned. It was however recognised that there would be no peace in Muskerry until one of them died.

Events now shook the Lordship of Ireland to its roots. The province of Ulster had been largely untouched by English rule but the government's grip was slowly tightening. To secure power the Crown depended on the cooperation of the ambitious and very able Hugh O'Neill, Earl of Tyrone. This man was exceptional among Gaelic chieftains, having strong Court connections, administrative flair and a keen interest in the latest military developments. Rather than rely on the old-fashioned gallowglas mercenaries, he equipped and trained his own clansmen in the use of modern weapons and manoeuvres. In 1595 he moved into open rebellion, initially to protect his own independence and his position as the paramount earl in Ulster, but the rebellion eventually became a national war of independence. By July 1596 his confederacy had issued a circular urging others, especially 'the gentlemen of Munster', to join them in defending 'Christ's Catholic religion' (Ellis 1985, p. 303). After the rout of the English forces at the Yellow Ford and the death of the English Marshall Bagenal, who led the force there, Dublin itself lay open to conquest in October 1598. After the rising in Munster the collapse of the Munster plantation took a matter of days; the undertakers fled, without supplying the militia that they had promised to maintain (MacCarthy-Morrogh 1986, p. 135). The land was reoccupied, unchallenged, by dispossessed former tenants of the Earl of Desmond (ibid., p. 133).

Queen Elizabeth realised the gravity of the situation; she appointed, against her better judgement, the neurotic Robert Devereux, second Earl of Essex, hero of Cadiz, to field an unprecedentedly large army of 17,300 troops against Tyrone (Ellis 1985, p. 306). In June 1599 Cormac Mac Dermot Mor went to meet Essex at Fermoy, offering his services, together with 200 kern (foot soldiers) all armed with pikes and muskets, as well as 100 cows for the army. Essex wore his forces out with futile sideshows and marches, then abandoned them after a shameful truce with Tyrone and dashed home to defend himself against charges of incompetence, disobedience and apparent treachery. Not long after Queen Elizabeth reluctantly had him beheaded when he attempted to raise a rebellion against her.

The next spring, after the expiry of the truce, Tyrone arrived in Munster, where the new Earl of Desmond, James Fitzgerald, joined his forces. They sent letters to all the southern chieftains expecting compliance and aid (Collins 1954, p. 4), but when the great army camped outside Blarney Castle the gates remained firmly locked. Cormac Mac Dermot Mor and his rival, Cormac Oge, avoided trouble by retiring to Cork City, but most of the southern chieftains, including other members of the Muskerry *derbfine,* came out in favour of Tyrone. To ensure their loyalty, Tyrone made them give up their young sons as pledges, a survival of the Gaelic custom of 'hostage-taking'.

The experienced soldier Lord Mountjoy replaced Essex as Lord Lieutenant. Against every expectation, a protracted war of attrition, ruthlessly employing 'scorched-earth' methods, gradually pushed Tyrone back onto the defensive in Ulster, while support for the confederacy in Munster withered under the assaults and bribes of the new President of Munster, Sir George Carew.

Tyrone had already pillaged Cormac Oge's lands, and on 3 May 1600 Carew ordered that Cormac Oge should 'enjoy the castle and lands of Kilcrea, the *tuath* of Kilcrea and other lands' (Collins 1954, p. 4) until such time as the dispute should be settled. Cormac Oge was to die only three months later, but his male relatives ensured that the feud rumbled on.

Things seemed to quieten down for a time in 1600. An incident indicates the new loyalties and style of chieftainship; when the O'Learys, vassals of the Lord of Muskerry, were the victims of a *creaght* by members of the Mac Carthy Reagh clan of Carbery. Some cattle were taken and the O'Leary chieftain and ten of his men were slain. Cormac Mac Dermot Mor would traditionally have been honour-bound to avenge this slight. However, he first asked permission of the Lord President. When this was denied he abided by the decision (Gillman 1892a, p. 34), a break with Gaelic tradition.

Despite these shows of loyalty and his written protestations to its chief ministers, the Crown did not completely trust Cormac Mac Dermot Mor. During this period Carew repeatedly asked Cormac Mac Dermot Mor to give him Blarney Castle as an English garrison. Equally persistently, the chieftain refused him with many excuses and explanations which, according to some, were the original 'blarney'. He had been threatened by Tyrone after he refused to join the confederate cause; many of his gentlemen and followers had been killed and he himself had been wounded. Then Teige Mac Cormac, younger brother of the litigious Cormac Oge, took up the rebel cause and was recognised as Lord of Muskerry by Tyrone and his main ally, Hugh Roe O'Donnell, in place of Cormac Mac Dermot Mor (Collins 1954, p. 6).

Cormac Mac Dermot Mor even went as far as sending the heads of slain rebels to Carew (ibid., p. 5) to prove his worth, but still Sir Robert Cecil wrote that Carew should 'make sure' of him. Carew meanwhile ensnared Cormac Mac Dermot Mor's brother and tanist, Teige Mac Dermot (of Castle Inch). Teige's son was 'in pledge' (a hostage) to Tyrone and he was in no position to be loyal to the Crown. The English also took hostages as pledges for good behaviour: Carew already had one of Cormac Mac Dermot Mor's younger sons in pledge. He also made sure that Cormac's heir, then a student at Oxford University, could not return to Ireland. Despite all evidence to the contrary, Carew was convinced that the vulnerability of his heir was the only thing that kept Cormac Mac Dermot Mor loyal.

Tyrone and O'Donnell had repeatedly asked for assistance from Spain, and on 3 September 1601, Philip III finally dispatched a force to Ireland. Although the cause was almost extinguished in Munster, Don Juan Águila's force of 3,400 experienced troops landed unopposed at Kinsale. The Spanish general judged his force too small to actively campaign and instead he fortified Kinsale while awaiting reinforcements from Ulster or Spain (Ellis 1985, p. 326).

Mountjoy was soon besieging the Spanish, assisted by the rising out of Muskerry under Cormac Mac Dermot Mor. This was a huge boost for the English, who gained a psychological advantage by marching the Irish forces past the Spanish trenches (Gillman 1892a, p. 34) prior to an attack. The English, however, had little faith in the loyalty of the Irish troops in the event of an English reverse. While the Spanish were uselessly imprisoned, Mountjoy went after O'Donnell in Tipperary and Cormac Mac Dermot Mor's force joined the march. Mountjoy's forces returned to Kinsale at the same time that Tyrone's relieving force arrived. Tyrone judged that he now had a fighting chance of defeating Mountjoy in the open field. The failure of his surprise attack at dawn on 24 October led to the destruction of the rebels. The Spanish had agreed to sally out when the Irish reached a rendezvous point, but because this point was never reached the Spanish stayed put and eventually surrendered under favourable terms (Ellis 1985, p. 326).

While the Nine Years War drew to a close, the war between rival Muskerry claimants escalated. Teige Mac Cormac, the would-be Lord of Muskerry, wrote a letter to the English alleging that Cormac Mac Dermot Mor had had various treasonable dealings with the confederates. He claimed that the chieftain was preparing to assist another Spanish expedition and to hand over Blarney Castle. As a result, Cormac Mac Dermot Mor was arrested and imprisoned in Cork, but Carew was now in a difficult position: if Cormac Mac Dermot Mor was executed, either Teige Mac Cormac would have to be recognised as Lord of Muskerry or he would cause further insurrection. Carew probably had little faith in Teige Mac Cormac's accusations, and Cormac Mac Dermot Mor's presence in Cork City as a prisoner was a constant source of trouble (Collins 1954, p. 7). Meanwhile there was still the problem of Blarney Castle. The official account of the war, *Pacata Hibernia*, records that

> his Castle of Blarney [. . .] is one of the largest and strongest castles within the province of Munster, for it is four piles joined in one, seated upon a main rock, so that it is free from mining, the wall being eighteen feet thick and well flanked at each corner to the best advantage.
>
> Considering therefore the difficulty that might grow in taking this castle by force, the President gave direction to Sir Charles Wilmot and Captain Roger Harvy (taking for their guard a sergeant with four and twenty foot) to make show of going only to hunt the buck in the parts near adjoining, and being hot and weary between the hours of ten and eleven o'clock in the forenoon, to take the said castle on their way homeward, and calling for wine and *usquebagh* (whiskey), whereof Irish gentlemen are seldom unfurnished, should, it were possible, themselves first and their soldiers afterwards, draw into the castle and gain possession thereof [. . .]
>
> [. . . the] strategem about the castle was frustrated; for the warders, whether out of the jealous custom of the nation in general (which is not to admit into their castles any strangers on their master's absence) or whether Cormock in his guiltiness had given them such directions, I know not, but sure I am that neither Sir Charles, though he much importuned to see the rooms within, nor any of his company were permitted to go into the gate of the castle nor hardly look within the gateway of the bawn. (Stafford 1896, p. 227)

Eventually Cormac Mac Dermot Mor, still in prison, signed a note authorising the handing over of Blarney to Carew, which was done without further incident. Despite this ultimate act of compliance, Carew decided to commit Cormac Mac Dermot Mor to the Tower of London indefinitely, 'until such time as the origins and depth of his offences, being found out, he might be brought to his trial according to due course of law' (ibid., p. 227). Carew also hoped to avoid unrest in Cork. He planned to send Cormac Mac Dermot Mor to the Tower on the night of 30 September 1602, but his plan was frustrated. A faithful servant, Maghon óg O Lyne (Lane), broke the window of the cell in which Cormac Mac Dermot Mor was held in Cork City, allowing him to escape despite 'irons and a guard to attend him' (Ó Murchadha 1985, p. 218). The chieftain was cut from his irons by a youth, Owen Mac Sweeney, who had climbed through the high window. McSweeney then pushed the understandably hesitant elderly chieftain from the window and he was caught unharmed below in an outspread cloak held by six other followers (Collins 1954, p. 8). The conspirators had a horse waiting outside the city walls to take him to Muskerry.

A plan was made to smuggle Cormac Mac Dermot Mor's heir out of England to safety in Ireland or Spain. John O'Healy, 'one of Cormock's old thieves' (Stafford 1896, p. 231), set out to England to find the young man. The faithful retainer was arrested on his outward voyage but managed to throw incriminating money and letters into the sea.

Cormac Mac Dermot Mor now decided it was time to act against his rival for the chieftainship, Teige Mac Cormac, who was holed up in Carrigaphooka Castle, to the north of Muskerry. Allied with Donal O'Sullivan Bere, the last great unsubdued chieftain in Cork, Cormac Mac Dermot Mor's supplemented forces took the tower house after a short siege. After this act of revenge, vital to his prestige, He applied to the council of Munster to grant him terms (Collins 1954, p. 8). On this occasion he had not asked the President of Munster's permission. On 31 October Carew wrote to the Privy Council of England that Cormac Mac Dermot Mor promised to remain a faithful subject for the rest of his life and that while he was 'deep in treason' he was only a 'juggling traitor' who had suffered enormous losses of goods and wealth. Sir Walter Raleigh, however, remained faithful to the memory of his former page, the now-dead disputed heir Cormac Oge, by urging the Queen not to accept the submission.

The ailing Queen 'took great hold' of her favourite courtier's assertions (ibid., p. 9), and she recommended that the Muskerry lands be split between Cormac Mac Dermot Mor and Teige Mac Cormac. Cormac Mac Dermot Mor had taken back the castle and lands of Kilcreaby after Cormac Oge's death in 1600, despite having made an undertaking to pass it to Teige Mac Cormac.

January 1603 marked a turning point: the Queen died and, despite Raleigh's opposition, Cormac Mac Dermot Mor had received a full pardon just three weeks before her death. Carew had evidently been won over by his old sparring partner. The chieftain was no doubt capable of great charm: only three years earlier, in May 1600, Carew had called this most 'cankered subject' a 'subtle fox' (Ó Murchadha 1985, p. 60). Another pardon awarded to Teige Mac Cormac ensured that the feud continued into the reign of the first Stuart king, James I.

The Nine Years War was effectively over and Tyrone started negotiations for a pardon which, incredibly, he received. Tyrone had started the rebellion in 1594 to protect his paramount position in Ulster and in this he was successful. Although Elizabeth had died six days earlier on 24 January 1603, Mountjoy concealed this fact from Tyrone (Ellis 1985, p. 311). O'Donnell died in Spain. Bloody 'mopping-up' operations continued for months in the far Gaelic west. The exceptionally hard-fought siege of Dunboy Castle, on the Beara Peninsula, ended in the massacre of its ward, but even this did not overcome the resistance of the O'Sullivan chieftain.

Carew cynically reported that the people of Cork, including in the cities, were falling over themselves in protestations of loyalty and contrition after learning of a victory they took no part in (Collins 1954, p. 6).

CHAPTER 7
The Seventeenth Century

THE NINE YEARS War in Munster had not distracted the Mac Carthys from their inheritance feud. Teige Mac Cormac (brother of Cormac Oge) still sought his inheritance, particularly the castle of Kilcrea. The heir of Muskerry, Cormac Mac Dermot Mor's son, another Cormac Oge (Fig. 5), eventually returned from his studies at Oxford and married a daughter of the Court-educated, Protestant Earl of Thomond. The Earl eventually became Lord President of Munster, a kingpin of the re-established Munster plantation (MacCarthy-Morrogh 1986, p. 171): a good man to have as a friend. The imposing but austere Kilcrea Castle became the home of the heir until his father's death.

After the death of Queen Elizabeth, Cormac Mac Dermot Mor continued to hold Blarney Castle but the sons and grandsons of his uncle Cormac Mac Teige continued their claims against him. In 1604 they had a minor victory: eighteen of Cormac Mac Dermot Mor's ploughlands were granted to them. He compensated for this by adding some confiscated O'Mahony lands to his estate. Teige Mac Cormac (Fig. 4) was never to live at Blarney as his father would have wished and had to content himself with the fortified house and lands at Ballea. (Ó Murchadha 1985, p. 60). This must be the oldest continuously inhabited house in Cork and still preserves its *yett* (iron grille) over the door.

The English-educated Cormac Oge became seventeenth lord in February 1616 in an uncontested succession; his father was buried at Kilcrea. The 52-year-old lord moved easily amongst both the new and Old English landholders and was able to protect his people from religious intolerance (Gillman 1892a, p. 35). In 1620 Muskerry was surrendered and regranted for a third time, to 'Charles, otherwise Cormac MacCarthy of Muckrumphe (Macroom), Knt' (Gillman 1892a, p. 35). His regrant underpinned a strange mix of old and new rights. He could demand from the tenants 'a complete number of labourers and *garrons* [. . .] who are also to answer and attend risings out and musters in the company of MacCarthy whenever he shall be called out by the crown or on any other legal course' (ibid.). The Mac Sweeneys continued in their role as gallowglas in return for the castle and lands of Mashanaglas. Macroom Castle, one of the clan's most important, was the lord's favoured home but the regrant underpins his ownership of Blarney (ibid.). What was 'legal' was up to him: he was still chieftain to his people.

The reestablishment of the Desmond plantations after 1603 drove many of the Gaelic chieftains who had survived the Nine Years War to ruin by means of the mortgage rather than the gun or scaffold. Cormac Oge's neighbour and distant kinsman, the MacDonogh of Duhallow, was a typical victim (MacCarthy-Morrogh 1986, p. 166). Cormac Oge was himself a prominent mortgagor who extended loans to his less astute countrymen in return for their lands – an activity usually the preserve of incomers, such as Sir Walter Coppinger, a Catholic Cork merchant of Danish extraction. His great lands and his exceptional control over his clan gave him an advantage he skilfully coupled with prudent estate management, mortgages, money-lending and careful husbandry. When he died his wealth was generally renowned (ibid., p. 185).

That wealth was probably mostly expended at Macroom rather than at Blarney. However, at some point a mansion house was built against Blarney Castle, recorded in a survey of 1654 as 'a new house of stone' (MacCarthy 1990, p. 162). This could have been built by Cormac Oge or by his father, Cormac Mac Dermot Mor. Cormac Oge was probably responsible for installing a fine stone 'Jacobean' fireplace in the first-floor chamber. A similar example in another Cork tower is dated to 1636 (Power 1997, p. 359). Enough remains of the mansion now to show that it was a multi-period structure.

In 1628 Cormac Oge was created Viscount Muskerry and Baron of Blarney and was an important member of the Council of the Confederation. The council represented the 'moderate' or royalist opposition to Parliament. Cormac Oge died in London in February 1640, where he was probably engaged in litigation, thereby escaping twelve years of civil war that nearly ended the lordship for good (Gillman 1892a, p. 35).

In 1632 Lord Strafford had been appointed Lord Deputy of Ireland by Charles I and was charged with reducing corruption and waste and increasing royal revenues. His mission apart, he had made himself intensely unpopular with all parties in Ireland by attacking them in different ways. The Protestant Earl of Cork Richard Boyle detested Strafford just as much as the Old English Catholics who were forced to pay fines because their 'graces' (freedom of worship) were not recognised (Beckett 1981, p. 65). Merchants and cloth manufacturers were enraged by new royal taxes. In all, rather than succeeding with his original 'divide and rule' policy he succeeded in uniting all the parties against him. He was recalled by Charles I in 1639.

Despite a period of remarkable social integration between the different parties in Munster, religion decided for or against rebellion in 1641 (MacCarthy-Morrogh 1986, p. 283). Those Irish who had been dispossessed as far back as the 1580s now saw their chance. As a contemporary Catholic source wrote in 1617: 'They will rather fight for their altars and hearths, and rather seek a bloody death near the sepulchres of their fathers, than be buried as exiles in unknown earth' (Cruise O'Brien 1972, p. 64).

Charles I's weakness and difficulties in England provided an opportunity for rebellion in Ireland, and also helped to precipitate civil war in England (Beckett 1981, p. 82). The rebels repeatedly declared their loyalty to the Crown. Some, such as those led by Sir Phelim O'Neill, sought a greater degree of independence and religious freedom, but others, especially in Ulster, took the opportunity to attack the new settlers in an attempt to reclaim their lost lands. In contrast, some of the English and Scottish settlers were sympathetic to the Parliamentary cause and the war in Ireland took on many of the colours of the English Civil War, with a few additional complications of its own.

Donogh Mac Cormac Mac Carthy, the eighteenth Lord and second Viscount Muskerry (Fig. 5), married a Butler; Elinor was the daughter of the Protestant eleventh Earl of Ormond. Donogh had been lord of Muskerry for a year at the outbreak of rebellion in 1641. After initially hesitating, he became one of the principle leaders of the Catholic cause in Munster. The Irish and Old English Catholic nobles were united by their religion (Beckett 1981, p. 37) but a fault line opened up with the landing in Ulster of Owen Roe O'Neill in 1642. He competed with the favourite of the Old English, their general Thomas Preston. Both had earned their reputations as soldiers in the Spanish Netherlands and neither accepted the other as superior; this division gravely weakened the Irish cause.

In the early years of the Civil War fighting was limited to occasional and scattered clashes and truces, neither side being able to gain a decisive advantage. The towns were strongholds of Protestant power while the country was overrun by Catholic forces. In 1642 Donogh Mac Cormac and the other Mac Carthys attempted unsuccessfully to besiege the Parliamentarian City of Cork, but a surprise attack broke through their camp's defences. In the same year the Confederation of Kilkenny was established, which represented Gaelic and Old English Catholics; Donogh became a member of the Council of the Confederation (Collins 1954, p. 86). The council represented the 'moderate' or Royalist opposition to Parliament.

Lord Ormond, Donogh Mac Cormac's brother-in-law, became Lord Lieutenant of Ireland in 1643 and headed the government forces against the Catholic insurgents. He was a leading opponent of the Confederation of Kilkenny. However Ormond gradually shifted from being the instrument of government to become the chief leader of the Protestant Royalist cause in Ireland, in a kaleidescopic conflict in which sides were continuously breaking, shifting and rearranging. By 1645 Ormond found himself negotiating with the Confederation on Charles I's behalf. The King offered greater freedom for Catholics in exchange for an army sent to England to support his cause.

During Ormond's negotiations in 1646 Blarney Castle was besieged and captured by Roger Boyle, Lord Broghill, acting under Ormond's commands (Cruise O'Brien 1977, p. 54). Lord Broghill was a son of Richard Boyle, the Earl of Cork, who was a family friend of the Mac Carthy Muskerrys. Cormac Mac Dermot Mor had even been godparent to one of Boyle's children (MacCarthy-Morrogh 1986, p. 278), despite their religious differences. Perhaps Broghill's knowledge of Blarney aided in its capture. However, the loss of Blarney did little to break Donogh Mac Cormac's power.

By this date the use of cannon made the more accessible castles such as Blarney impossible to defend. Only those in remote situations without good roads remained useful. The lack of cannon damage to the tower suggests that no more than a token resistance was made. Broghill may well have sent the ward of Blarney a 'paper bullet' of the sort posted to Cahir Castle (Co. Tipperary) by Cromwell:

> Sir – Having brought the army and my cannon near this place according to my usual manner in summoning places, I thought fit to offer you terms honourable to soldiers: that you may march away with your baggage, arms and colours, free from injuries or violence. But if I be, not withstanding, necessitated to bend my cannon upon you, you must expect the extremity usual in such cases. To avoid blood, this is offered to you by
> Your servant,
> Oliver Cromwell (Cruise O'Brien 1977, p. 64)

Having captured it, Broghill made Blarney his headquarters (de Breffny 1977, p. 54) and the castle escaped the normal burning and 'slighting'.

Ormond's treaty with the Kilkenny Confederation was published in July 1646. This was immediately undermined in August that year by Archbishop Rinuccini, the papal legate. He had come on a mission to the Confederation in October 1645 and had stayed at Macroom Castle for a week (Collins 1954, p. 86) as the guest of Donogh Mac Cormac Mac Carthy. At the synod in Waterford in 1646 he denounced the treaty and said anyone who supported it would be excommunicated. Although the landowners and magnates were prepared to risk this, the ordinary people, including the soldiers promised to the King, were more susceptible to clerical influence (Beckett 1981, p. 97) and the peace treaty collapsed. Lord Ormond passed over his command, including Dublin, to Parliamentary forces, regarding them as the lesser of two evils (ibid., p. 99), and then departed Ireland in July 1647.

The situation then escalated until Oliver Cromwell arrived in August 1649. Cromwell's Ironsides embarked on a new conquest of Ireland. Where there was opposition the war was prosecuted without mercy. The capture of Drogheda was followed by the massacre of its garrison.

Cork City opened its gates to Cromwell's forces in November 1649 but verses celebrating the presence of Cromwell and Ireton, his son-in-law, at the siege of Blarney can be dismissed (Fitzgerald 1899, pp. 16–17). The other Muskerry strongholds were not taken until 1650, when Donogh Mac Cormac's forces were defeated at Macroom on 10 May by Broghill's army (he was now a Parliamentarian). Carrigadrohid and Carriganamuck castles were also captured (Gillman 1892a, p. 36) as well as Kilcrea (Collins 1954, p. 86). Carrignamuck become a Parliamentary garrison.

Donogh Mac Cormac returned to Muskerry to raise a relieving force for Limerick City, then besieged by Ireton, but he finally surrendered at Ross Castle, Killarney, in May 1652 after utter defeat near the Blackwater River. His forces surrendered on articles that left the officers free to take service abroad and to carry recruits with them (Beckett 1981, p. 103). By the summer, Ireland was entirely under the control of the English Parliament.

The General Parliamentary Act in 1652 dictated that rebels who, like Donogh Mac Cormac, had 'borne command in Ireland against the English' should be exiled and two-thirds of their estates forfeited. The Act allowed that 'lands to the value of the other third should be assigned to their wives and issue' (Gillman 1892a, p. 36). This in practice forced the Irish westwards, taking poor land in Connaught in 'exchange' for the remaining part of their ancestral lands. There is some evidence that, exceptionally, Donogh Mac Cormac's wife was allowed to stay at Blarney (ibid.). General Ludlow, to whom Donogh Mac Cormac had surrendered, apparently made an undertaking to allow this. Donogh Mac Cormac went abroad (see below). Lord Broghill, after changing his allegiance from Charles I to the Parliamentarians, later became a supporter of the Restoration of Charles II and championed the restoration of the Lord of Muskerry, though he had been the chief agent of his downfall.

The Irish 'rebels' were for the most part Royalists. The victory of the Protestant-led Parliamentary party led, amongst other things, to the final destruction of the Gaelic social system throughout Ireland. The eventual recovery of the Muskerry lordship in the last decades of the seventeenth century was an exceptional feat of political skill and good luck. The shaky edifice of the lordship did not, however, survive to the end of the century.

Donogh Mac Cormac joined the exiled court of Charles II in Flanders, and his heir, Cormac, commanded the Muskerry regiment in the French service (McCarthy 1965, p. 7). 'Don Jean de Morphie' (Murphy) was the colonel of an Irish regiment in Flanders in the wars of 1646 to 1659. In his will of 1669 he requested that his widow should go and live in Blarney, because a cordial invitation had been made by 'my lady, the Countess Dowager of Clancarty' (Elinor Butler, widow of the second Viscount). The Murphys were loyal retainers to the Mac Carthys (Ó Murchadha 1985, p. 247).

Lord Broghill sensed that the Commonwealth would not outlast the ailing Cromwell and he was amongst those who began negotiations for the restoration of Charles II in 1657, a move almost solidly approved in Ireland. In an unlikely turn of events, Donogh Mac Cormac returned with Broghill, now Lord Orrery, to Ireland in 1660. Ormond too was restored as Lord Deputy of Ireland, and was given the unenviable task of restoring order and implementing the king's generous promises of restitution of forfeited lands. This was especially difficult as he was much distrusted in Ireland, including by Donogh Mac Cormac (Barnard and Fenlon 2000, p. 181). The Acts of Settlement in 1662 and the Act of Explanation of 1665, the latter promoted by Ormond, attempted to restore some lands to original owners. This forced some adventurers (those who had loaned money to Charles I in exchange for Irish land) and former soldiers to give up the lands they had acquired. The Act of Explanation was not successful in meeting all its commitments and was dictated by expediency rather than strict justice (Beckett 1981, p. 120).

The Mac Carthy Muskerry clan chieftain now sported the new title of Earl of Clancarty, while his heir took the title of Viscount Muskerry (Fig. 5). The Act of Settlement in 1661 restored 'Donagh E. of Clancarty and Charles (Cormac) Viscount Muskerry (his son) to their blood and honours, and for investing and settling them in their several estates' (Gillman 1892a, p. 36). In

1665 Donogh died, just after a new patent confirmed his restored estates, which was recorded in a certificate in 1666 (*Records of Ireland*, 1825, p. 240). Not all those specifically named in the Act of Explanation had had their estates restored.

The first Earl's death resulted in inheritance difficulties (Fig. 5). His son Cormac, the dashing Viscount, left the French Army at the Restoration and served in the Royal Navy against the Dutch as a volunteer officer under his old companion the Duke of York, Charles II's brother (Gillman 1892a, pp. 36–7). He married the daughter of the Earl of Clanrickarde but predeceased his father, killed in action on the *Charles*. His three-year-old son inherited the title of Earl from Donogh Mac Cormac but then also died (McCarthy 1965, p. 9).

Callaghan, the first Earl's second son, had joined a seminary in France and was intended for the priesthood. His appearance as the heir to Muskerry caused some gossip and uncertainty about his status, although he had apparently not actually been ordained.

Lord Broghill (Earl of Orrery) was as high in favour with Charles II as he had been with Cromwell. The rather colourless Callaghan (Charles) had, despite his priestly training and Jansenist beliefs, married Elizabeth, a daughter of the Earl of Kildare. This marriage had been arranged by Ormond and Orrery, her guardian. The new Countess was a staunch Protestant; her grandfather was the Earl of Cork. Dublin gossip that Elizabeth had married an ordained priest infuriated her (ibid.).

Donogh Mac Cormac Mac Carthy, or Lord Clancarty, had done his best in his 1665 will to provide for the relatives who had lost all their lands as a result of supporting him in the Civil War. Some of these former freeholders were eventually reinstated as leaseholders (Collins 1955, p. 4), but Callaghan, the third Earl, died in 1676, at the age of 43, perhaps worn out by litigation. Although a settlement with the freeholders was eventually reached, the estate was encumbered by debt. The aggrieved parties included Cromwellian soldiers, who had been granted land in Muskerry during the Commonwealth. Sir William Penn, the Quaker and subsequent founder of Pennsylvania, was amongst their number (McCarthy 1965, p. 8, n. 6).

Callaghan's widow was anxious that their eight-year-old son, Donogh, the fourth Earl (Fig. 5), should be brought up a Protestant and he was therefore transferred to Oxford University at a tender age. There he was placed in the care of his tutor, Dr Fell, whose name is still recalled in the rhyme:

> I do not like thee, Dr Fell,
> The reason why I cannot tell,
> But this I know, and know full well,
> I do not like thee, Dr Fell.

At the age of 16 the young Earl gave Dr Fell the slip and married Elizabeth Spencer, the daughter of the Catholic Earl of Sunderland (Collins 1955, p. 3). It amused Charles II to connive in the elopement of young Donogh. His uncle Justin Mac Carthy then smuggled him back to Blarney, where to the delight of his kinsmen he announced his conversion to the faith of his ancestors.

This Indian summer of the Mac Carthys of Muskerry was soon to end, however, when they again chose to join the losing side. The friendship between the first Earl, his son Cormac and the Duke of York was to prove their undoing, as the family maintained its loyalty to James II. The militia of the town of Bandon had committed atrocities during the Civil War and had been one of the first towns in Munster to declare for Cromwell. When the Duke of York inherited the throne from his brother in 1685 and became James II he took revenge, removed the town's charter and garrisoned it against its will.

Resentful of this treatment by James, the citizens were roused to expel the garrison when they heard the news of the arrival of William of Orange in England to depose James. James was still King, however, and the garrison was restored by the forces of the royal administration represented by Major-General Justin Mac Carthy and the Earl of Clancarty (Collins 1955, p. 75). Their regiments of O'Briens, Dillons and Mac Carthys still had something of the rising out about them.

In February 1689 William of Orange was proclaimed King at Westminster. On 12 March the exiled king James II landed at Kinsale, where he held his court, and the next day he lodged in Cork at the town house of the Earl of Clancarty, the nephew of his old friend Cormac. James had now moved his operations to Ireland, where his Catholicism was less of a problem. He called an Irish Parliament, and the spirited 20-year-old Earl accompanied him to Dublin to sit in the House of Lords. His loyal service caused him to travel the length and breadth of Ireland: he led a regiment at the siege of Derry (Co. Londonderry) and held Elizabeth Fort in Cork City, where he was taken prisoner after the city capitulated in 1690 (ibid., p. 76).

After the Battle of the Boyne Donogh Mac Carthy and his peers were branded traitors and outlaws by the winners, much as forty years previously. Donogh was imprisoned in the Tower of London but eventually escaped in a manner fit for an historical romance. To conceal his absence, he made up his bed to appear occupied and placed his periwig block (a dummy head of wood) on the pillow. He escaped to France where he joined James's court at Saint-Germain-en-Laye, which was supported by James's cousin Louis XIV.

During this period Donogh made a bigamous marriage, which ended with the death of his second wife. In France he began to pine for his first wife Elizabeth Spencer, who had been a child when he married her in 1684. Donogh slipped secretly back to England to renew his first marriage at Elizabeth's father's house. Unfortunately he was betrayed and committed to Newgate Prison. An agreement was made that his mother could visit him regularly and his wife was allowed to see him at all reasonable hours.

King William, a connoisseur of handsome young men, was as taken with 'that little spark Lord Clancarty' as Charles II had been (Collins 1954, p. 76), but it was politically impossible to reverse the attainder, and in the circumstances Donogh was lucky to escape with his life. A pardon was granted only on condition that he was exiled for life and his lands forfeited. He received a pension of £300 yearly. With this he apparently retired to Hamburg and purchased a small island in the mouth of the river Elbe. He made a living from salvaging wrecks and died there on 22 October 1734, aged 64. He had two sons, Robert, Lord Muskerry, a captain in the English Navy and, Justin Mac Carthy, Esq. The unfortunate Lord Muskerry was suspected of having Jacobite sympathies and was struck off the list of naval officers in 1749. As a result, he, like many others, entered foreign service (Crofton Croker 1824, p. 304).

Blarney Castle's days as a symbol of Gaelic rule were over. Silence fell in its halls. The last official poet of the Mac Carthys of Blarney was Tadhg Ó Duinnín. He lamented the defeat and dispersal of the Gaelic nobility after 1691. He knew his days as a bard were over, and he ended the lament with the couplet:

> Mo Cheárd ó mheath le malairt dlíghe I nÉirinn,
> Mo chrádh go racha gan stad le bríbhéireacht.
> My craft being withered with change of law in Ireland
> O grief that I must henceforth take to brewing. (Ó Murchadha 1985, p. 139)

With Blarney's demise, the bardic school of Blarney also came to an end, although some of its traditions lingered for a while in the locality (Corkery 1924, p. 110).

Huge sales of the forfeited Irish lands belonging to James II's followers were carried out at Chichester House, Dublin. No Catholic was allowed to bid. It was government policy to ensure the lands had English owners so concessions were made so that purchasers had to pay only one-fifth of the purchase money in cash (Collins 1955, p. 77). The lordship first carved out by Dermot Mor, son of the King of Desmond, was knocked down for sale on 6 November 1702 'for one-fifth in money, rest in debentures' (Gillman 1892a, p. 37).

CHAPTER 8

The Jefferyes and the Colthursts

All the Clancarty estates were forfeit in 1692. Elizabeth, the Dowager Countess Clancarty, acting as trustee for her son, Donogh, had already leased the Blarney estate to Rowland Davies, the Dean of Ross and Cork, in 1679 (MacCarthy 1990, p. 162). The extensive Clancarty lands were divided up into various parcels, the largest extent of which had been granted to William Bentinck, the son of William III's favourite, the Earl of Portland (Collins 1951, p. 19). The land 'around' Blarney was sold early on to the Hollow Sword Blade Company of London, an industrial company which was heavily involved in Irish forfeiture sales (Lewis 1837, Vol. 1, p. 211). It is not clear whether the Blarney estate itself formed part of this sale since it is also listed in the *Book of Posting and Sales* as having been sold in the major sale of forfeited estates at Chichester House in Dublin on 26 October 1702. It is described as including 'the village, castle, mills, fairs, customs and all the lands and park thereto belonging, containing 1,401 acres'. At the time of the abortive sale, to a Mr Sweet, the tenant, Dean Davies, was noted as paying £360 a year and was apparently living in the castle. In 1876 Richard Caulfield was told by Sir George Colthurst that the Dean 'had been ejected' (MacCarthy 1990, p. 164) but there is no contemporary evidence for this. It was said that when the Dean left for Dawstown he removed the oak rafters from the castle and used them in Dawstown House (ibid.). However, eighteenth-century alterations to fireplaces and brick repairs in the tower suggest that the rafters must still have been in place then and the building in use.

The Blarney estate, apparently now comprising only 917 acres, was successfully sold to Sir Richard Payne or Pyne, the Lord Chief Justice of Ireland, for £3,800 in April 1703 (ibid.). Apparently Sir Richard then became uneasy because of rumours that Lord Clancarty would be reinstated and decided to sell the estate almost immediately (Mulcahy 2002, p. 8). It was purchased in 1703 or 1704 for £3,000 by Sir James Jefferyes, the Governor of Cork City.

Sir James, the new owner of Blarney and ancestor of the current owner, was born in Scotland, probably in 1635, and spent much of his life as a soldier in Europe. He had been some years in Poland, as captain of the guard to King John III, who knighted him in 1676. He was later British Resident at Danzig. He lived for a long time in Sweden and had two wives, both Swedish; the first bore him five children, the second four. He came to Ireland as part of William of Orange's army of English, German, Dutch and Danish troops, who first drove James II out of England to Ireland and then pursued him to defeat at the Battle of the Boyne. Jefferyes was appointed Governor of Duncannon Fort. He brought his second wife and children to Ireland, probably after William had gained full control of the country and it was largely at peace (ibid.).

In 1698 William III appointed Jefferyes Governor of Cork City. In 1700 he had a pay award of 20s per day, backdated to May 1699, payable until March 1704. This seems not to have been paid, since in 1704 he petitioned Queen Anne to pay the arrears, an amount in the region of £1800, pointing out all his loyal service to her brother-in-law. He claimed to have spent all he had. She replied by granting the post to him and his heirs for seven years ('Notes and Queries' 1911, p. 35). Accommodation seems also to have been a problem since he received a grant of £20 a year from the Corporation of Cork for lodgings. At around this time he bought Blarney Castle. In 1703 he became MP for Lismore, Co. Waterford, and continued as MP until 1714 (Burke 1970, p. 614).

Sir James's eldest son and heir spent a great deal of his life abroad and was seldom at Blarney until his retirement. In 1701, at the age of 25 or 26, James Jefferyes went to Sweden as secretary to the British Envoy at Stockholm, Dr John Robinson, in a post which his father had obtained for him (Notes and Queries 1914, p. 156). His father also purchased a commission for him in 1704, but Captain Jefferyes did not actively pursue this career. The young Swedish King Charles XII was involved in fighting the Great Northern War to ensure Sweden's continuing independence. From 1707 he fought a campaign against his main enemy, Russia, then ruled by Peter the Great. Exceptionally, James Jefferyes was allowed to go with him, officially as a volunteer but in fact as a combatant military attaché with an allowance from the British Treasury (Mulcahy 2002, p. 11). After his defeat at the battle of Poltova in 1709 Charles XII went into exile in a Moldovan village called Bendery, then in the Ottoman Empire. Jefferyes was captured and imprisoned by Cossacks but eventually managed to return to London in late 1709 or early 1710 and presented the Treasury with a bill for £248 for the losses incurred during his experiences (ibid.).

James Jefferyes did not rejoin Charles XII until 1711 so he may have spent some time at Blarney in the meantime. In 1715, after the death of Queen Anne, Jefferyes's appointment as Ambassador to Sweden was confirmed, but he left the Swedish Court, which was still in exile, in 1717.

Returning to London, he married Elizabeth Herbert, a widow. His stay in London was short – by the autumn he was en route to Moscow, where he became Resident at the court of Peter the Great. He left behind his wife, who apparently bore him twin daughters, Louisa and Elizabeth, and died shortly afterwards (ibid., p. 20). Jefferyes remained in Moscow until Britain changed sides, when he became Ambassador to Danzig and the Hanse Towns. He appears to have married again there and there is some confusion whether his daughters were borne by this unnamed wife or by Elizabeth Herbert (Burke 1970, p. 614).

In 1721 Sir James Jefferyes died and Captain Jefferyes inherited the estates; the Corporation of Cork made him a freeman of the city in 1722 but he seems not to have been tempted to stay in the county. His diplomatic career continued: in 1727 he was reappointed Ambassador to Moscow by George II and remained there some years (Mulcahy 2002, p. 28). In 1732 he was back in the British Isles and married Ann Broderick, the daughter of Lord Middleton, whose father had been Chancellor of Ireland (Burke 1970, p. 614). She bore him three sons, two of whom did not reach adulthood. He did not enjoy retirement for long but died in 1740, once again abroad.

Blarney was then inherited by six-year-old James St John Jefferyes. He held Blarney until his death in 1780. His tenure is best known for the industrial expansion in the village. There is an interesting description of this in *Arthur Young's Tour in Ireland* (1892). Young, an English agronomist, visited the estate in 1776 and described the newly built town. It consisted of an inn, a new church and 90 houses. Mr Jefferyes had rented plots of land to industrialists and allowed them to build their own mills and factories on them. With a grant from the Linen Board, which had been trying to encourage the linen trade in the county since 1711 (Cronin 1993, p. 736), and money from other government bodies, Jefferyes also built some mills himself. When Arthur Young visited there were 13 mills with different functions, including a bleaching mill, a stamping mill for printing patterns on cloth, a stocking factory, a woollen mill, a broadcloth mill, a leather mill, a bolting mill, a paper mill and a tape manufacturer. Mr Jefferyes had spent about £20,000 (including government grants) on developing the village and adding facilities such as the church and bridges. A cotton mill was also built. Jefferyes was, Young thought, 'a good businessman as well as a benevolent landowner' (*JCHAS* 1911, Vol. XVII, p. 35). He was making considerable profits, for land that had previously yielded £6–10s (£6.50) an acre in rent was worth £113–15s (£113.75) an acre by the time the stamping mill was built. There was a benefit to local agriculture too, since increased demand brought higher prices for meat and dairy foods. This period saw the beginning of a tradition of woollen mills at Blarney which has lasted more than two centuries (Reilly 1948, p. 33).

Although Young does not mention it, James St John Jefferyes also improved the grounds of the castle and laid out ornamental gardens influenced by the Italian designer Garzoni (Hillyard 1954, p. 71). It was he who planted trees among the boulders, laying the foundation of the romantic landscape that began to attract visitors in the late eighteenth century (Chapter 9). James St John married Arabella Fitzgibbon, a barrister's daughter whose brother, John, became Attorney-General, then Lord Chancellor and the first Earl of Clare. Jefferyes sat as Member of Parliament for Middleton in the Irish Parliament between 1758 and 1776 (Burke 1970, p. 614). He died in 1780 (Donnelly 1983, p. 40), leaving Arabella to pursue an active widowhood.

Mrs Jefferyes became one of the leaders of the Rightboys or Whiteboys movement in Cork, although she often denied this. This secret society, which acted under the orders of a mythical 'Captain Right', was active in 11 counties in Munster, Leinster and Connaught (ibid., p. 2) especially during 1785 and 1786. It was chiefly a revolt against the payment of tithes to the Church of Ireland. These tithes were payable in kind rather than money, and farmers from the largest to the smallest were asked for a tenth of any crop they produced. The amount due was assessed by proctors employed by the Church. The Rightboys society harassed various members of the Protestant clergy and their proctors. With the relaxation of the penal laws in the 1770s the Catholic Church was also allowed to demand a regular system of support from the population, which was an added burden to the poor, and, to a lesser extent, the Catholic Church was also a target for the Rightboys.

While the Rightboys' resistance to tithes appeared to be an effort by the poor to resist a tax which further pauperised them, contemporary writers knew that the movement had great support amongst the gentry, including Mrs Jefferyes and her friend Sir John Colthurst. In a pamphlet published in 1787 Bishop Woodward of Cloyne pointed out that the poor were demanding an end to tithes on hay, a wealthy farmer's crop, rather than tithes on potatoes, chief crop of the poor and their sustenance (ibid.). The gentry would thus benefit considerably if the movement succeeded. However, Mr John Bennet, a Cork apothecary and a staunch Protestant who wrote an account of the Rightboys for his children, was more inclined to see the revolt as a religious/sectarian matter (ibid., p. 14) and an attack on the established Church.

Bishop Woodward was also keen to portray the Rightboys as 'a Popish mob' (ibid., p. 3), but the fact is the movement's strategy was dictated by a number of leading Protestant gentry, and Mrs Jefferyes was a leading member 'of the internal cabinet of the Whiteboys republic' (ibid.). It seemed easier for critics to believe it was a Catholic plot to bring down the established church than to suggest openly that the gentry had exploited popular discontent to benefit themselves through reduced tithe payments. A Capuchin friar and pamphleteer Arthur O'Leary sat on the fence, scolding the Rightboys for their attacks while at the same time writing 'a perfect hymn of praise to Arabella Jefferys [*sic*]' (ibid., p. 6). He compared her to Zenobia, the Queen of Palmyra who opposed the Romans, in that she had 'a manly heart in a female breast' (ibid., p. 42). Mrs Jefferyes's connections to the heart of the Irish establishment may have made her a particularly fearsome opponent.

There was a further twist when the Catholic population in a number of parishes, including Blarney, deserted their churches and began to worship instead in the Protestant churches, apparently encouraged by Mrs Jefferyes (ibid., p. 14). It was claimed that Catholic clergy were charging high fees to perform weddings and other rites. Mrs Jefferyes, says Mr Bennet, was certainly 'remarkably active' in this matter: 'she frequently headed the rabble to Blarney church, wrote several letters to different people on the subject of ecclesiastical dues'. She went to Dublin to personally harangue Dr McKenna, a 90-year old 'prelate', on the subject and also wrote to several parish priests, dictating what fees they should take for marriages. However, Mr Bennet, something of a conspiracy theorist, believed that Mrs Jefferyes and others wanted everyone to believe that the country people wished to free themselves from 'the alleged oppressions of the Romish priests as well as the established clergy' (ibid, p. 18).

Although contemporary commentators were inclined to see the matter along polarised religious lines, it is interesting to note that this was an issue where two different classes (Protestant gentry and Catholic tenants) had shared economic interests and a common objective: to reduce their tithes. Mr Bennet hints, perhaps correctly, at a broader attack on all organised religion (ibid., p. 14). This was the age of the Enlightenment, and on the cusp of the American and French Revolutions freemasonry and other secret societies flourished as well as a strongly anti-clerical current in political and social thinking, which may have influenced the Rightboys movement.

The lake excavation at Blarney coupled with other incidents, caused unease in the neighbourhood. On 25 June there was a public announcement in Mallow that the Whiteboys of the parish would appear early next day at Blarney and should get horses ready. The rector of Mallow was visited at midnight by 100 people, who demanded his horses. It was said that 2,500 men assembled the next day at Blarney. The events were reported in a local newsletter, 'Flyn's Paper', provoking a letter to the paper from the parish priest at Blarney, apparently written under Arabella's dictation. He claimed 'for three months past no armed, disorderly, or disguised persons whatsoever were on or in the town or lands of Blarney' (ibid., p. 20). If this muster was simply for the work on the lake, it nevertheless caused considerable suspicion and fear of revolt. In another incident at about the same period Mrs Berkeley, a rector's wife, was requested to send horses and men to Mrs Jefferyes at 'Captain Right's' request. Mrs Jefferyes denied all knowledge of Captain Right and told Mrs Berkeley that the work on her estate was being done 'by the kindness of her neighbours' (ibid., p. 21); shortly after this the work was discontinued.

Mrs Jefferyes gave up her Rightboys activities at this point, probably warned to do so by her brother, John Fitzgibbon, a prominent MP at the time. Fitzgibbon, who became Attorney-General in 1783, was a firm upholder of the establishment with a very conservative outlook, and his sister was presumably causing him some embarrassment. Shortly afterwards some Catholic bishops delivered a rebuke to local Catholics saying that they should not try to right grievances through riotous behaviour and secret oaths (ibid.) and the movement seems to have lost momentum from that point.

It is interesting to note that one of Mrs Jefferyes's close friends and colleagues during the Rightboys revolt was Sir John Conway Colthurst, Baronet of Ardrum, who appears to have been one of the chief instigators of the movement. He was described by Mr Bennet as 'a man of polished manners and insinuating address' but also 'subtle, vindictive, and cruel and of a nature sordidly avaricious' (ibid., p. 12). Fiercely anti-clerical, he believed one could say or do as one liked as long as one was prepared to risk one's own life for it; like others in that period, he regarded duelling as the appropriate way to resolve matters of honour. In February 1787 he was mortally wounded in a duel by Mrs Jefferyes's brother-in-law, Dominick Trant: Colthurst had challenged Trant for making slighting remarks about him in an anti-Rightboys pamphlet (ibid., p. 12). The grandson of Colthurst's brother Nicholas would ultimately marry Mrs Jefferyes's granddaughter Louisa, and together they would inherit Blarney.

Mrs Jefferyes continued to fight wrongs in other spheres. Her family background had obviously given her the opportunity to discuss legal matters since her childhood. By the beginning of the nineteenth century she had successfully undertaken a number of property lawsuits ('Notes and Queries', 1895, p. 82), including one for a Captain Menzies that she had been advised by her brother not to pursue, as she could not win it. Nevertheless she did, and Captain Menzies regained his estate.

Mrs Jefferyes was also active on the domestic front. She devoted time and energy to improving the decor and facilities of Blarney House, the Gothick mansion rebuilt by her late husband beside the castle. In 1797 it was reported in John Harden's *Tour* that 'Mrs Jefferys [*sic*] is modernising the domestic apartments and has enriched and added some splendid rooms [. . .] they are in some state of progress and promise well without hurting the great original' (MacCarthy 1990, p. 163). A portrait painter, J.D. Herbert, who visited her at Blarney apparently in the early nineteenth century, gives a picture of country house life and entertainments of the time which, Mrs Jefferyes's legal activities apart, would fit neatly into a Jane Austen novel. Herbert was 'greatly struck with the antique character of the building and the magnificently surrounding scenery' ('Notes and Queries' 1895, p. 82).

In contrast to the exciting era of Mrs Jefferyes the next two Jefferyes owners seem to have done relatively little to attract public attention. Mrs Jefferyes's son, George Charles, a captain in the dragoons as a young man, was best known for presenting a petition to the King (George III) in 1800 against the dissolution of the Irish Parliament and legislative union between Britain and Ireland. One may guess at some family friction here, since one of the major promoters of the union was his uncle, John Fitzgibbon, 'the greatest unionist of all' (Beckett 1981, p. 272), who since becoming Lord Chancellor in 1789 was effectively the most powerful man in Ireland. Fitzgibbon's major policy was the defence of the Protestant ascendancy; he believed this was best done by linking Ireland more firmly with Britain (ibid., p. 235). The petition had been signed by the freemen of the City of Cork and others, but was unsuccessful ('Notes and Queries', 1911, p. 36). George Charles married Anne La Touche, daughter of an important Dublin banking family, who died in 1798 leaving him a son.

It was during George Charles Jefferyes's tenure of the estate that the Blarney mansion burned down. This happened in 1820 or 1821, and there was a vast auction of what we would now call 'architectural salvage'; all the good building materials were sold off. The statues were bought by Sir Thomas Deane, a well-known Cork architect. Since a great many wooden items, such as window frames, doors, floorboards and so on, were sold off too, the mansion must have been damaged by the fire rather than totally destroyed (MacCarthy 1990, p. 163). There was some restructuring of the Blarney estate during the 1820s, which involved the eviction of some of the cottiers and those who occupied sub-divided farms (John Mulcahy, pers. comm.).

With the end of the Napoleonic War in 1815 there was an industrial decline in Cork; the textile industry was particularly vulnerable to cheaper, English-made goods (Fahy 1993, p. 794). A real slump occurred in the years after 1825 (Cronin 1993, p. 737), apparently exacerbated by the removal of protective duties and a lack of capital, leading to insufficient mechanisation in Ireland. A number of visitors to Blarney in the nineteenth century commented on the derelict state of the village, compared with the thriving picture presented by Arthur Young in the previous century. The general decline was noted by Crofton Croker in 1824:

The alteration struck me forcibly. In 1815, I remember a large square of neat cottages, and the area, a green shaded by fine old trees. Most of the cottages are now roofless; the trees have been cut down, and on my last visit, a crop of Barley was ripening in the square. (p. 291)

One visitor in 1830 was Count Charles de Montlambert, who attended mass in the 'Catholic chapel at Blarney' which, he noted, had 'no seats, no decoration, not even pavement' (Anon 1951, p. 22). However, it was enlarged and repaired in 1835 and described as 'a very neat edifice' (Lewis 1837, p. 212). The writer Fr Prout described the village as 'a sad ruin' in contrast to the beauties of the castle, but for the recent establishment of a spinning factory (Mahony 1836, vol. 1, p. 35). This was presumably the Blarney Woollen Mills run by the Mahony family, established in the town in the early nineteenth century (Reilly 1948, p. 36); it employed about 120 people at this period, spinning and dyeing woollen yarn (Lewis 1837, p. 212). Another observation made after the Famine (1859) noted that the town square, which had once had a statue, was now 'yellow with corn' (Brewer 1825–6, 379).

Despite the terrible impact of the Famine throughout the West of Ireland in particular, the village of Blarney seems to have escaped the worst of it. In June 1847 the *Cork Examiner* described Blarney as an 'OASIS' in the 'surrounding desolation' (John Mulcahy, pers comm). Later in the year the *Examiner* reported that at a harvest home in Blarney the parish priest claimed that no one had died of famine.

There are a number of factors that contributed to this, chiefly the existence of alternative employment, off the land, for local people. The two sources of work were the Mahonys' wool spinning factory and the railways that were then under construction. Clearance of the poorest tenants (referred to above) in the 1820s meant that the Blarney tenants on the whole were the more prosperous sort. In December 1846 a Captain Gordon reported to the Board of Works that '[a]bout Blarney [. . .] some farming is going on', in contrast with other areas where even farmers were applying for outdoor relief (Mac Suibhne 1997, p. 149). The local people may have benefited from the fact that the Mahony family, who ran the Blarney Woollen Mills, were active on the relief committee. They arranged delivery of a soup boiler to their depot in Cork, cutting out bureaucracy that might otherwise have delayed relief. There is also a story that part of the mills were converted to grinding wheat to relieve distress in the area (Reilly 1948, p. 36). It is well known that elsewhere the slowness of the arrival of the relief was a major contributor to the number of deaths. The availability of local charity probably meant the most desperate people could avoid the truly grim conditions of the recently built workhouse in Cork City, which deterred all but the absolutely destitute from flinging themselves on its mercy. The conditions there and the spread of diseases such as cholera resulted in appalling death rates in the workhouse. In this period there was a certain amount of assisted emigration but in 1849 only one person from the Blarney electoral district left with the workhouse's assistance (O'Mahony 2005, p. 150), which confirms the picture of Blarney as an area that largely escaped the worst of the Famine.

The role of the Jeffereyes is not well-documented; there is one minor, rather regrettable, episode related in the *Cork Examiner* in November 1847; St John Jefferyes, one of the presiding magistrates at the Blarney Petty Sessions, fined a woman from Inniscarra 20s. Her crime was to 'pluck up a single turnip' from a field belonging to his son-in-law, Sir George Colthurst of Ardrum.

St John Jefferyes was the last male Jefferyes. He married Harriet Taylor and they had one child, Louisa Jane, who married Sir George Conway Colthurst, Baronet of Ardrum, Inniscarra, in 1846 (Burke 1970, p. 614). Louisa and Sir George inherited Blarney on her father's death in 1862. Not totally sedate, St John also had an illegitimate son, named 'St John George of Paris', who was educated at Eton and died in 1896 (ibid.).

Henry Colthurst, a Yorkshireman of property in 1460, is the first Colthurst recorded in *Burke's Peerage and Baronetage*. His descendants began to come to Ireland with the nobility in the sixteenth century and probably benefited from the outcome of the Nine Years War, which ended in 1602.

Henry's grandson Matthew had either become very wealthy or had gone to Court and made himself useful to Henry VIII, since he acquired a good deal of property after the dissolution of the monasteries. When Mary I restored Catholicism he became Treasurer of Ordnance in 1554, but the family do not seem to have remained Catholic much longer. He was connected with Wardour Castle in Wiltshire but his eldest son, Edmund, moved further west to Cornwall and died after 1611. His third son, Andrew, accompanied Sir Walter Raleigh to Ireland and was granted lands there, but he apparently retired to Somerset. It is interesting to speculate whether he knew Cormac Oge Mac Carthy, the claimant to Blarney Castle who joined Raleigh's entourage in the late 1580s and whose claim was supported by Raleigh for some years. Another son, Thomas Colthurst, also went to Ireland and was granted the castle and manor of Shane and other lands (Burke 1970, p. 613). Thomas's third son, John, remained in Ireland and was killed there in 1607. John had two sons; the younger, Edward, was a vicar in Wiltshire who died around 1599 and whose eldest son, Christopher, settled in Cork and lived in Ireland until he died in 1641 'murdered by rebels near Macroom' (ibid.).

Christopher's son John Colthurst of Coolevissanally died in about 1682; he is, presumably, the John Colthurst listed as being given a grant of lands in the Acts of Settlement of 1662 and the Explanation of 1665 (O'Hart 1887, p. 455). His son, another John, of Ballyally, was granted lands in Co. Cork under the Commission of Grace, which settled a wide variety of land disputes, usually in favour of the newcomers, in August 1684. His son Colonel Nicholas Colthurst of Ballyally was High Sherriff of Cork in 1736; he had had two daughters and on his death his brother John Colthurst of Ardrum became head of the family. He was MP for Tallagh from 1734 to 1757 and also had what seems almost to have been a statutory year as High Sherriff of Cork in 1738.

His son John Conway Colthurst of Ardrum was the first Baronet; he was MP for Doneraile from 1751 to 1760, MP for Youghal from 1761 to 1768 and MP for Castle Martyr from 1769 to 1775. He was created a baronet of Ireland in August 1744. In 1741 he married Lady Charlotte Fitzmaurice, daughter of the Earl of Kerry, and he died in 1775. His son St John Conway was the second Baronet, the Rightboys instigator, and friend of Mrs Arabella Jefferyes (discussed above). When he was killed by Arabella's brother-in-law in a duel, he was succeeded by his brother Nicholas. Nicholas Colthurst followed a family pattern of becoming High Sherriff of Cork (1788), MP for Johnstown, Co. Longford, from 1783 to 1790 and for Castle Martyr from 1791 to 1795 (Burke 1979, p. 614). He married Harriet La Touche, a member of an important Dublin banking family. Their son, Nicholas, who succeeded to the title in 1796, was born in 1789. He was educated at Eton, then joined the Army during the Napoleonic Wars as a captain of the Cork Militia, then a captain of the 68th Foot Regiment.

This Nicholas Colthurst was MP for Cork City from 1812 to 1829, a period of interesting class conflict. Rival landed families, such as the Colthursts, Kingstons, Hares and others, treated Cork City as their own battlefield. In addition they tended to patronise the citizens. They set up a 'county club' to which only 'gentlemen' were admitted – however 'gentlemen' was defined, the club did not admit those in trade. There was a feeling amongst the merchant classes, both Protestant and Catholic, that they needed to gain some access to power for themselves, and one of them, Gerard Callaghan, a Protestant convert and former MP for Dundalk, Co. Louth, attempted to break the landowners' power base. He stood against Sir Nicholas Colthurst in the 1820 elections but failed to defeat him. In the next decade Callaghan and his brother Daniel 'spent an estimated £30,000 on (election) contests in Cork city' (d'Alton 1993, p. 765) and finally won the seat in 1829, the year Sir Nicholas died. He was married to Elizabeth Vesey and was succeeded by his eldest son.

George Conway Colthurst, the fifth Baronet, was born in 1824 and educated at Harrow and Christ Church College, Oxford. In 1846 he married Louisa Jane Jefferyes, and thus, in due course, succeeded to the Blarney estate on the death of her father in 1862. He was variously ADC to the Lord Lieutenant of Ireland, a Justice of the Peace in Co. Cork and MP for Kinsale from 1863 to 1874. He died in 1878.

The sixth Baronet, George St John Colthurst, was born in 1850. He was in the 43rd Foot Regiment and was ADC to the Lord Lieutenant of Ireland. He married Edith Morris and was succeeded by two sons, one after the other. He was involved in investment in the railways and was a keen cricketer (ibid., p. 760). He inherited Blarney at a politically polarised time, because of the growth of support for Home Rule and he held it throughout the upheavals of the War of Independence and the Civil War.

The 1880s were difficult times for the landowning classes and indeed for anyone connected with the land. Many landowning families lived beyond their means and rents were inadequate to meet their expenses. In the 1860s the government had instituted the Encumbered Estates Courts, which investigated heavily indebted estates and, in some cases, sold them off. The agricultural slump of the 1880s made it difficult to increase rents. The rise of the Land League, with its demands for the '3 Fs': fair rents, fixity of tenure and freedom for the tenant to sell their occupancy (Beckett 1981, p. 390), led to boycotts against unfair landlords, as well as protests in favour of Irish independence. A major uniting force for the unionists was the Primrose League, which Sir George was involved in. This movement, in which many of the women from landowning families took a leading role, seemed to perform a social function as much as a political one; it has been described as 'tea-and-cakes conservatism' (d'Alton 1993, p. 770). It is certainly true that a garden party held at Blarney in August 1891 drew rather more participants than a major political meeting that same year in Cork. The garden party attracted about 600 guests and was extremely well organised – d'Alton suggests that 'the gentry could be relied upon to put on a good show'. The *Cork Examiner,* cited by d'Alton (d'Alton 1993, pp. 770–1), described the organisation:

> The open-sesame to the proceedings was a perforated ticket, one part of which carried the holder over the Cork–Muskerry line, another admitted to the grounds, and the third entitled to refreshments. (ibid.)

The British Government continued to reform land ownership in Ireland bit by bit; later on the 1903 Land Act enabled the Government to buy all Irish land that was let to tenants (Burke 1958, p. xviii). The tenants in turn were able to buy this land back from the government. This meant that absentee landlords who had let most of their property were left with very little land, only the land they farmed themselves. After this the average estate was reduced to about 300 acres.

Despite all the changes in Ireland during the twentieth century, the Colthursts weathered the storms of the War of Independence and the Civil War and held onto Blarney, unlike many other Anglo-Irish families, who relinquished their estates and moved to England. But we should not give the impression that Blarney was a tranquil spot to live in between 1916 and 1923. It is well beyond the scope of this book to discuss the complexities of this period. The loyalties and passions that engaged people during the Civil War in particular still reverberate today, but it is interesting to record some of the events of that period which affected Blarney.

The Captain of the IRA's Blarney Company was Frank Busteed, whose memories of the period have been recorded. He had been employed at the Blarney Woollen Mills, which had a strongly Republican workforce (Hart 1998, p. 210) and he joined the Fianna in 1910. In his memoir he describes an early incident involving Blarney Castle:

> In 1917 an American priest came to Blarney with a group of Americans. They had a tricolour up on Sunday and they were madly Irish. They went to Blarney Castle and they stuck the tricolour up on top of the Castle and Sir George Colthurst rang the police and told them to remove it. A dozen of us went up to see what was wrong. We saw 4 or 5 Yanks and the RIC men beating the devil out of them, and this man, the priest O'Shea, was on top of the sergeant. We came out suddenly from a place they didn't expect us to be in. I hit Sgt Doyle and knocked him down the stairs, the

stone steps of the Castle. The RIC ran away and we wanted to get out of the village. Dan Buckley [. . .] and I rushed for the Barracks but some of the RIC closed the door on us. They had the priest inside. We then beat up the police outside and after that I was foul of the police. There had been raids for arms and after that my house had been picked out for special attention.

[Later we] raided Colthurst's house. We thought they would open the door for us, but they wouldn't. We found rifles, 15 revolvers, shotguns and bags of ammunition. McAuliffe and I were coming home at 5 in the morning when we stood to chat at the crossroads. I heard steps up the village, but a special raiding party from the Barracks was busy, and I could hear them banging on my door. I was on the run. I got Colthurst's gun, which was a good one, and I carried it with me. McAuliffe, who had a gun also, was on the run. That raid took place in July or August. (O'Malley notebooks)

The Civil War broke out after the signing of the 1921 Treaty with the British which partitioned Ireland and established the Free State. Those who had fought together in the War of Independence were divided between the Free Staters and the Republicans. According to Frank Busteed: 'Of my men, very few joined the Free State, but quite a lot of the men went neutral. But all the fighting men, save one or two, stayed loyal' (O'Malley notebooks). Cork City was a stronghold of the Republic, opposed to the Treaty. When the Sinn Féin Ard Fheis was due to be held in 1922 most of the Cork branches mandated their delegates to vote against the Treaty, but the Blarney Sinn Féin Club mandated its delegates to support it (Mulcahy, in prep.).

Blarney's farming community was suffering both from the imposition of martial law, which banned fairs and markets, and from transport disruption due to the destruction of bridges and roads (ibid.). In early 1922 the farmers cut wages, causing farm workers in the Cork area to strike for about two weeks. A court of arbitration, under the auspices of the Dáil Éireann Department of Labour, upheld a 15 per cent cut in wages but ordered the farmers to employ as many people as they possibly could and to settle wages for the rest of the year by 25 March.

The Blarney estate also had some problems, since it still had many tenants (these farmers had not bought their farms when they were enabled to do so by the 1903 Land Act). The tenants requested a rent reduction because of the economic difficulties they were experiencing. This request was refused and the tenants then decided not to pay any rent until a settlement was reached. The estate responded by bringing a bankruptcy proceeding against the leader of the tenants, J.F. Corcoran. At the same time there was a nationwide movement of evicted former tenants of estates who were claiming back their old homes. A public meeting in their support was held in May 1922 in the grounds of Blarney Castle. The meeting called upon the government to arbitrate. Across the country there were a number of cases where landowners were intimidated, with guns or kidnappings, burning of buildings and the driving off of livestock, into giving up their lands to former tenants or their heirs (ibid.). This happened in Blarney, reported in the *Cork*

Examiner (Mulcahy, in prep. *Cork Examiner* 19 May 1922): '[T]he occupying tenants were evicted by armed force, and other persons put in possession of their farms.' This intimidation was condemned by the Republican authorities who controlled the area at the time, and a number of people were jailed. Policing at this period was carried out by local IRA units, a body known as the Irish Republican Police, and IRA officers acted as magistrates in the Republican courts.

In August 1922 the Free State took Cork from the Republicans and a few days later they established a base in Blarney. Free State soldiers took over a house in the square and soon afterwards were attacked by the Republicans, who were helped by the cover of the surrounding woodlands. Another attack came at night two days later, when a bomb was thrown from the church grounds into a house where soldiers were believed to be. This was followed by an exchange of fire. Bullet holes can still be seen in the walls of village houses (ibid.). There are a great many stories of bodies being found but no documentary evidence supports these.

Skirmishes in Blarney continued right up to the end of the Civil War, with the Republican forces led by Frank Busteed and the 'one-eyed gunner' Con Healy. Such was local Republican enthusiasm that even after the end of hostilities, when the Republicans had been told to lay down their arms, there were two further incidents. On 21 June 1923 the telephone lines into Blarney were cut and two nights later the army post was the target of sniper fire (ibid.).

Having survived these events with his estate intact Sir George St John Colthurst died in December 1925 and was succeeded by his sons, first George Oliver, the seventh Baronet, and then Richard St John Jefferyes, the eighth Baronet. Both were educated at Harrow and Trinity College, Cambridge, and both fought in the First World War. George was a captain in the South Irish Horse and won a Croix de Guerre; later on he served in the Intelligence service. Richard was a captain in the London Regiment (Burke 1970, p. 613). George studied law at Cambridge. He was MFH of the Muskerry Hounds (1930–44) and limped slightly from a hunting accident (van Hoek 1948, p. 25). He never married and died in 1951. His brother married twice, first Cecily Cholmondeley in 1911, with whom he had two daughters, and then, in 1927, Denyse West, the mother of the ninth Baronet. His eldest son, Richard La Touche Colthurst, married Janet Wilson-Wright in 1953 and had four children; he succeeded to the title in 1955, the year the present baronet, Charles, was born. Charles took over running the estate in 1986 and succeeded to the title in 2003; he is married with four children. He has concentrated on developing the forestry on the estate, as well as developing tourism at the castle.

CHAPTER 9

The Blarney Stone and Tourism

WHICH CAME FIRST, the legend of the Blarney Stone or the castle's appeal to tourists? The two are intimately linked. Blarney with its ruined castle and, after 1821, the ruined mansion beside it, its picturesque grounds, rivers and the wooded Rock Close, was and is a beautiful place to visit. The original attractions were the pleasure grounds and the local landscape. Rock Close 'is so exquisitely beautiful that no just idea of its influence over the feelings can be conveyed by the tameness of prosaic description' (Brewer 1826, vol. 2, p. 377).

Later 'the picturesque valley of the Sournagh, which may be likened to a Swiss ravine' (Mahony 1898, p. 128), was regularly praised in travel books. The ornamental grounds, with rocks arranged in a naturalistic way into a series of features, were laid out by James St John Jefferyes in the mid eighteenth century. It is not clear whether any of the rock groupings there pre-dated Jefferyes's work, but a number of names, such as 'Witches' Kitchen', 'Wishing Steps' and so on, were attached to these groups, suggesting greater antiquity and a connection with Druids. Jefferyes had visited Europe and seen various styles of garden, which may have influenced him. The exact date of their construction is not known, but there is a large flat stone carved with 'G. Jefferyes 1759' (Hillyard 1954, p. 71), presumably the date of birth of his heir, which covers the wishing steps. Rock Close became extremely atmospheric once the trees had matured. This owner of Blarney had had a keen eye for the picturesque. A mansion house had been built beside the castle, perhaps as early as the sixteenth century, but it was certainly there by 1654 when it was recorded in a Cromwellian survey. The house was updated periodically, casemented timber windows were added and so on, but it was in James St John Jefferyes's time that it was completely rebuilt as a four-storey house in Georgian Gothic style. When this house burned down in 1820 or 1821, the overgrown house ruins were described as 'a picturesque adjunct to the keep'; however, they have since been 'tidied up' (MacCarthy 1990, p. 164).

The castle and its surroundings delighted those with a yearning for mystery, awe and even horror. The Blarney grounds are described by Francis Mahony ('Father Prout') as 'a romantic cavern and an artificial wilderness of rocks' (Mahony 1836, p. 35). The Rock Close was also endowed with mysterious associations with Druids, witches and fairies that perfectly accorded with Romantic sensibilities. How authentic these associations are is debatable, but they were all likely to appeal to the growing interest in both the medieval and Celtic culture, then mysterious to the foreign visitor. The lack of real knowledge or understanding of traditional Gaelic clan culture at this period led to Blarney being misunderstood as a medieval feudal castle of the type that featured in *Ivanhoe* (O'Hegarty 1950, p. 22) and elsewhere in popular literature. This taste for the antique was nurtured in the novels and verse of Walter Scott and the spurious 'Ossian' poetry cycle. Nevertheless, Blarney was far from the only picturesque ruined tower house in Ireland. Within a few miles of it there are several, including the eerie Kilcrea Castle near the similarly ruined Friary. Blarney's development as a tourist attraction was due to a number of factors, the most significant being its situation, its proximity to a major city, Cork. Here there was an urban population with sufficient disposable income to take the occasional 'outing', at first in outside jaunting cars and carriages; later on, tourism increased with the growth of the railways.

The Gothick taste was for darkness, ruins, dungeons, stories of death, ghosts, thwarted love, and a sense of antiquity. Gothic novels by writers such as Mrs Radcliffe, Matthew Lewis and Horace Walpole provided, amongst other things, antiquarianism in a fictionalised form. Jane Austen parodied such novels in her juvenile novel *Love and Freindship*' (sic) and mocked their influence on young women in *Northanger Abbey*. Many popular spots could supply ruins, beauty and atmosphere, and what could not be supplied in the way of legends, mystery and tradition might be created through the development of stories which, while thrilling, were not necessarily factual. In a castle there had to be dungeons and other grisly features to inspire imagined horrors to heighten the visitors' enjoyment. If no authentic dungeon existed, for example, the label might be applied to any suitable-looking dark place, such as a store room or cistern chamber. Many of the traditions at Blarney, including the links with Druids, seem to have arisen at this period.

Blarney was not the only ruin in the British Isles with atmosphere, but it had a very particular attraction. The French Consul in Dublin, Charles Etienne Coquebert de Montbret, was appointed Consul of Ireland by Louis XVI and continued in this role even through the French Revolution. His records cover every aspect of life throughout all of Ireland (Kennedy 1952, p. 62). He made one of the first known mentions of the Blarney Stone's power in an account of a 1789 tour of Ireland:

> Blarney Castle on the top of which is a large stone that visitors who climb up are made to kiss, with a promise in so doing they will gain the privilege of telling lies for seven years. (Pettit 1989, p. 25)

Crofton Croker, on his 1824 visit, observed that

> [t]he military and historic recollections connected with Blarney are doubtless of sufficient importance to give an interest to the place: but to a curious superstition it is perhaps more indebted for celebrity. A stone in the highest part of the castle wall

is pointed out to visitors, which is supposed to give to whoever kisses it the peculiar privilege of deviating from veracity with unblushing countenance whenever it may be convenient – hence the well-known phrase of 'Blarney'. (p. 305)

Although eloquence is now generally agreed to be the gift of the Blarney Stone, beliefs were vaguer in the early days and in 1805 an English visitor recorded that

[a]bout four miles before we reached Cork on our left, my fair *compagnon du voyage* pointed out to me Blarney Castle upon a turret of which there is a stone which is very nearly *inaccessible* and possesses, it is said, the rare virtue of making those for ever happy who touch it. (Carr 1805, p. 408)

As Pettit comments, the practice of kissing the stone seems to commence with the improvement of Blarney, with extensive ornamental grounds and plantations, in the 1770s. The success of this programme is reflected in the 'Groves of Blarney', the celebrated satirical ballad by Richard Millikin, written in 1799. This poem was a parody both of a similar paean of praise to another castle and of the style of English written by the hedge schoolmasters of his day (Kavanagh 1994, p. 174) and was often performed as a 'comic turn'. Nevertheless, Kavanagh quotes Padraic Colum as saying 'the structure and sound of Gaelic poetry are reproduced in it; the "a" sound of "Blarney" is woven through every stanza' (ibid). Despite apparently listing all Blarney's attractions, the ballad does not mention the stone. This was made good by a later Irish writer Francis Mahony, a priest who took the pen name 'Father Prout', who added the following verse in 1835:

There is a stone that whoever kisses,
Oh! He never misses to grow eloquent.
Tis he may clamber to a ladies' chamber,
Or become a member of parliament.
A clever spouter he'll soon turn out or
An out-an-outer 'to be let alone'
Don't hope to hinder him, or to bewilder him
Sure he's a pilgrim from the Blarney Stone. (Mahony 1835, p. 38)

Different writers stress different forms of eloquence that may be achieved by kissing the stone: success with the opposite sex, in politics, with one's creditors and in litigation, or in any situation where a persuasive tongue might prove useful. 'Eloquence' was regarded by some writers as a euphemism; it was described as 'a stone said to have the power of imparting the unenviable privilege of hazarding without a blush, that species of romantic assertion, which many term falsehood. Hence the phrase *Blarney,* applied to such violations of accuracy in narration' (Brewer 1826, vol. 2, p. 377).

The stone's powers were often treated with disdain, since the idea of becoming an able liar was morally unattractive. Nevertheless the tradition gave a visit to Blarney Castle a focus and an objective – Fr Prout was not the only writer to describe visitors as 'pilgrims'. The other attractions might decline (in 1860 *The Tourist's Illustrated Hand-book for Ireland* declared that the Rock Close and 'the enclosed pleasure grounds' had suffered from neglect but 'could be restored' (*The Tourist's Illustrated Hand-book for Ireland* 1860, p. 106)), but the Blarney Stone suffered no loss of popularity.

What then is the Blarney Stone? True believers will be shocked to hear that the stone which is currently kissed is not the stone always believed to have been *the* stone. Most of the legends and commentators refer to a stone 'high up in the tower'; this seems to have been conflated with an often-quoted date stone, once visible on the north-east angle, with the inscription '*Cormach Mac Carthy Fortis Mi Fieri fecit* AD *1446*' (Black 1857, p. 151). This was notoriously inaccessible, so the thinking was clearly that anyone bold enough to reach it deserved a reward. Other candidates too have been recognised. In 1836 the antiquarian Windele wrote:

> On the highest part of the north-east angle, to which a flight of half a dozen steps leads, is placed a stone inscribed with the date '1703'. This is generally pointed out as the far-famed impudence-conferring 'Blarney Stone', to kiss which has been the object of many a pilgrimage, in order to participate of its marvellous powers and properties. [. . .] But a doubt hangs over the identity of the stone. Whilst that which we have spoken of has generally been pointed out, the Revd Mr Horgan, the parish priest of Blarney, and a gentleman of high antiquarian character, strongly denies its title, and asserts that the real stone is to be found in the face of the wall at the north-east angle, within eight feet of the summit of the castle. To reach which the pilgrim must help himself with rope and tackle, and be lowered *head downward* to enjoy the advantage of kissing it. As few have nerve enough to attempt the feat at such a dizzy height, we would ask how those who have honoured the stone of '1703' have come by the honied and glib tongues they are invariably known to have carried away with them? When this is satisfactorily answered we will adopt the worthy priest's opinion – but not 'till then. (Windele 1839, p. 235)

After a visit by the Royal Society of Irish Antiquaries Arthur Hill reported in 1893 that the Blarney Stone formed the sill of one of the machicolations on the south side of the castle (Anon. 1893, p. 340). This stone was allegedly damaged during Broghill's siege of the castle and was cramped with iron to secure it. However, previously a 'waterworn hollow stone' on the east side was known as *the* stone in Hill's father's time. There was also another stone said to be carved with a shamrock which was 'supposed to possess special virtue', but sadly this was 'in an inaccessible place, known to few' (ibid.). In an amusing account of a Victorian visit, *A Little Tour in Ireland* by Dean Samuel Reynolds Hole, John Leech's 1858 woodcut (Fig. 6) clearly shows the north-east 'waterworn' stone as the young ladies' target (Hole 1859, p. 225). Leech was a well-known

Fig. 6 The Blarney Stone *(showing the north-east stone and two ladies who have just kissed it), woodcut by John Leech (repr. Hole, 1859, opp. p. 228). [British Library. © British Library Board. All right reserved. Shelfmark 10930.b21 Licence no. 1022251.041]*

illustrator who worked for *Punch* and illustrated works by Dickens and Surtees. This book was published after a fortnight's trip to Ireland by artist and author and is now chiefly of interest for Leech's work, Hole's creaking humour not having stood the test of time (Rose 1950, p. 32).

It appears from this that the parapet of the north-east lookout turret was lost, perhaps deliberately, for safety reasons. Reverence was transferred to the present stone. The first mention of this was in 1888: 'The situation of the stone has shown a tendency to vary according to the predilections of the guides. But that now exhibited is the lowermost of those clasped between the iron bars as shown (on the north face) in the engraving' (Lockett 1888, p. 102). This is the lintel that supports the machicolation between the third and fourth corbels (Fig 33), mentioned by Arthur Hill above. The reinforcement was probably added to counteract damage caused by souvenir hunters. Lockett was, however, aware of the tradition that identified the 'real' Blarney Stone as the date-stone on the north-east angle.

The fabulous unpublished account given by 'the Bard of the Lee', John Fitzgerald, attempts to explain this transference. He credits the Jefferyes with finding

> the loose stone of the battlement (which was disturbed by the first cannon shot from the besiegers commanded by Broghill), knocking about the top of the great tower. This was undoubtedly clamped with iron and placed in its present position by the order of Sir James Jefferyes, as the date 1703 cut on it proves, the purchase of the estate being made by Sir James in the year 1701. (Fitzgerald 1899, p. 16). The estate was actually purchased in 1703 or 1704.

Although Arthur Hill and John Fitzgerald agree on the cause of damage to the lintel (Cromwellian guns), this too may be a traditional story rather than a fact, as there is a complete lack of cannon damage to the rest of the castle. The damage may simply be due to souvenir hunters. Although antiquarians remained aware of the connection of the stone with the 'watch-tower, on the parapet of which is the celebrated 'Blarney Stone'' (Coleman 1895, p. 23), the general public soon forgot about its shift in position.

In 1899 very few amongst the thousands of visitors dared kiss the stone because the safety bars now below it had not been put in place. In any case, Victorian morality would have made it out of the question for women to adopt the kissing position now required. A scaffold and platform existed for a time, and made it possible for ladies to kiss the stone from below without (much) risk to their modesty (Fitzgerald 1899, pp. 16–17) but the present arrangement of bars is twentieth century.

The inaccessibility of the Blarney Stone is significant in one of the early versions of its story. The common factor in all the Blarney Stone legends is the idea that the stone was unlike any other. There is no superficial evidence that the stone is petrologically distinct from any of the others making up the tower. It appears to be limestone, although Dean Hole (describing the former stone) describes it as 'a conventional granite. [. . .] Very accessible for osculation' (Hole

1859, p. 225). In *The Reliques of Father Prout* the earlier stone is described as 'a certain stone of a basaltic kind, rather unusual in the district [. . .] placed on the pinnacle of the main tower' (Mahony 1836, p. 35).

The myths of the Blarney Stone all suggest it came from a different source than the rest of the building materials and many suggest it was inserted into the castle wall subsequent to its building. Various legends account for the stone. It was once known as 'Jacob's Pillow', brought back from the Holy Land after the crusades. A slightly more plausible tradition relates that one of the Mac Carthys provided Robert Bruce with 5,000 kern (infantry) to fight Edward II in Scotland. As reward he received a piece of the Stone of Scone, on which the kings of Scotland had been inaugurated. A third story records that Cormac Laidir Mac Carthy, the reputed builder of Blarney, rescued an old woman from a river, who turned out to be a witch. In thanks, she told him of a magic stone that already formed part of his castle and instructed him to mount the keep and kiss a certain stone in the wall (Hillyard 1959, p. 8). The plot here, a danger overcome before a gift is received, is typical of many folk tales.

There are also mythical elements to the story; it is believed that some actual remnants of paganism survived into Ireland into the thirteenth century (Simms 1987, p. 27). The story of the Blarney Stone could conceivably contain a description of the type of inauguration ceremony that kings would have undergone in pagan Ireland, albeit in somewhat garbled form. No account of the Mac Carthy kings of Desmond's ceremony exists, but some other Irish kings were inaugurated next to a holy well, the ceremony presided over by a thinly disguised sovereignty goddess Eithne (ibid., p. 28), later transformed into the archetypal hag/wisewoman. Some of these elements are hinted at in the longest, most elaborate explanatory myth, M.M. Buckley's 'The Old Legend of Blarney', which combines fairies, Druids and chieftains; perhaps this somewhat gory tale was meant for children, as the old woman's role is taken over by a beautiful fairy. In this version a powerful Druid living in the eighth century has two daughters, Cleena (Cliodhna?) and Aoival. Cleena is exceptionally eloquent and beautiful and is the 'Queen of the Fairies in South Munster' (p. 3). She falls in love with a young chieftain who is 'fighting to free his native land' (p. 5) but her love is not reciprocated. Nevertheless, after he is killed in battle she finds he has fallen on a stone on the side of the Lee, into which his blood has soaked. She spends many hours there weeping and kissing the stone and her magic gifts are somehow transferred to it.

This legend is continued by Robert Gibbings in his book *Lovely is the Lee* (1945). In his version Cormac Laidir is worrying about some litigation he has got involved in and a forthcoming court case. Cliodhna, Queen of the Fairies, tells him to kiss the stone he will see facing him when he first wakes up and goes out: 'a stone that has been brought from the banks of the Lee'. He duly does so and wins his court case. He then carries the stone to the top of the castle and hides it so that no one else will be able to match him in eloquence.

The connection between Blarney and smooth talking goes back probably to the sixteenth century. Francis Mahony supports Crofton Croker's theory that when Cormac Mac Dermot Mor Mac Carthy (the sixteenth chieftain) was asked to surrender Blarney to Lord Carew so that it might be used as an English garrison during the Nine Years War he kept making promises and excuses, protesting his loyalty to the Crown but never delivering the castle to the English (Mahony 1836, vol. 1 p. 35). This apparently made Carew something of a laughing stock with his colleagues and the phrase 'Blarney talk' became proverbial at that time.

Was Cormac Mac Dermot Mor's charm the origin of the idea of 'blarney'? It is at this point in history that the word 'blarney', with the meaning of 'persuasive talk', is thought to have come into the English language. Queen Elizabeth I is supposed to have said, on receiving another self-justifying communiqué from Cormac Mac Dermot Mor, 'Blarney, Blarney, I will hear no more of this Blarney!' (de Breffny 1977, p, 54). There *may* be a kernel of truth in this story. But there is another possible, complementary, derivation. Aenghus nan-Aor was a 'bard' or versifier who died in 1617. His satirical *Tribes of Ireland* recounts his mistreatment at the hand of various chieftains and nobles. The charge of inhospitality was the worst that could be made against anyone in Gaelic society. He wrote:

> Flattery (*bladmahd*) I got for food,
> In great Muskerry of Mac Diarmada,
> So that my chest died [dried] up from thirst.
> Until I reached Baile an Cholaig. (O'Daly 1852, p. 64)

The Royal Irish Academy's *Dictionary of the Irish Language* gives the Irish original of that quatrain as using the word '*bladhmann*' not '*bladhmahd*' which normally means 'boasting, bragging, complacency' (Quin 1990, col. 111). In John O'Donovan's note (6) to the quatrain he offers the translation of 'blarney, bland talk', so it is possible he suggested that a kind of pun was intended (Dr Katharine Simms, pers. comm.).

It could be that an itinerant hungry bard rather than the Queen of England was responsible for associating Cormac Mac Dermot Mor with cajoling but occasionally insincere charm. It is worth pointing out that traditional etymology says that 'Blarney' is an anglicisation of '*Blárna*', a diminutive of '*blár*', a field, so 'Blarney' means 'a little field'. However, this is apparently an unusual word, and although it can be found in Irish and Scottish Gaelic dictionaries it has not been found in general use ('Notes and Queries', 1912, p. 53).

Whether people came to Blarney for the stone or for its scenic beauty, early tourism to Blarney was something of an elite activity. The sort of people who toured Ireland in the early nineteenth century were usually wealthy and fashionable. The famous visit to the stone by Sir Walter Scott with his friend and fellow novelist Maria Edgeworth in August 1825 is mentioned by many writers (Mahony 1836, p. 36) and Windele:

> Foremost and distinguished by one and all, the worshippers who have approached it, was the Northern Ariosto; Sir W. Scott, who on the 9th August 1825 accompanied by his gifted son-in-law Lockhart, Miss Edgeworth, &c. paid the homage of his worship. (Windele 1839, p. 235)

Obviously a visit by the most popular writer of his day gave Blarney cachet as a tourist destination. It became a standard part of the traveller to Ireland's itinerary, just as Rome formed part of the Grand Tour. The Romantic movement, with its love of mountains, dramatic scenery and (relatively) inaccessible places, made tourism in the most impressively scenic areas of the British Isles popular with the educated classes. The early visitors to Blarney were drawn from this class. The Napoleonic wars in the early nineteenth century essentially made the rest of Europe 'out of bounds' for British travellers who turned their attentions to more local sights. The 'craze' for dramatic scenery may seem surprising nowadays, but with no mass travel and no mass media to depict such sights, actually beholding Blarney, or any other famous site, made an intense impression on visitors. Nineteenth-century writers refer to visitors to Blarney as 'pilgrims'; and it is interesting to note that until that period pilgrimages were the nearest thing to mass tourism that European culture had produced. It was the railways which eventually brought mass tourism to Blarney, a few years after Walter Scott's visit.

Before the railways visitors would come to Blarney in a carriage or by horse and cart. The 'outside jaunting car' was popular in the late nineteenth century, despite competition from the railways. It could take a more picturesque route and, of course, drive through areas inaccessible to the train.

The railway age began for Blarney in 1849, when the Great Southern & Western Railway opened a station at Blarney on the line that connected Cork and Dublin, about one and a half miles to the east of the castle. It was in fact the first station to be built on the route (Phelan 1997). This line connected Blarney not only with the two major cities but also with their ports, where tourists arrived, keen to visit Ireland. From this point onwards there were rather more visitors to Blarney, especially Americans and other foreigners. In 1853 the *London Journal* wrote: 'Scarcely any part of Ireland has gained more celebrity than the far-famed village of Blarney' (quoted in Newham 1992, p. 49).

However, these visitors were still relatively affluent travellers; mass tourism had yet to take off. But with the arrival of another railway line Blarney reached a peak of popularity at the end of the nineteenth century.

The fame of the stone spread to America, and offers were made to the Colthursts for it – one allegedly as much as £100,000. One promoter wished to remove the stone for exhibition at the World Fair of San Francisco. When refused he made the best of it by instead quarrying many tons of stone from nearby and cutting it up for sale as souvenirs, claiming it was from the same quarry as the stone used to build the castle (Ward Lock and Co. 1950, p. 71).

In 1883 the Tramways Public Companies (Ireland) Act was passed, which enabled local promoters to build small lines suitable for tram engines on minor routes. A company was formed to build a line covering the Cork, Coachford and Blarney areas. This was designed partly to promote tourism in the area and partly to provide a goods service for agricultural produce going into Cork and essential goods, such as fuel and dry goods, going to the rural stations. After some false starts the line was promoted by the Cork & Muskerry Light Railway Company with tourism very much in mind. They had rented some land from Sir George Colthurst and a Mr Sherrard, and were involved in preparing the castle for greater tourism. The Blarney grounds were embellished and fenced (Newham 1992, p. 10), the castle and caves were opened to the public six days a week from 9.00 am to 7.30 pm, at a charge of 6d. Train passengers would be admitted at half price and admitted to the grounds directly through the station. It appears that the railway promoters had now undertaken to exploit the castle as well as the tramway. This synergy between tourist attraction and railway helped profits and 'special trains' were provided to take visitors to events such as the Primrose League Garden Party in 1891 (Ch. 8).

Work began in February 1887 and the Blarney line was given priority to enable the line to be opened in time for the autumn tourist season. It was ready in the summer and the Board of Trade inspection declared 'it was the best 8½ miles of permanent way he had seen on any tramway' (Newman 1992, p. 11)) There was a gala opening on 4 July – ladies and gentlemen travelled up the line, visited the castle and enjoyed champagne and claret. It was then open to the public on 8 August 1887.

The railway, and presumably the outing to the castle, was immensely popular; the company's shares performed well; more rolling stock had to be acquired to meet demand; and, with one or two slight setbacks, the whole enterprise succeeded brilliantly until 1914. In 1891 an extension line was built to Donoghmore, and Lady Colthurst cut the first sod. In contrast to the earlier part of the line, which had been constructed in the teeth of fierce local opposition, this section was actually built by popular demand. Sir George Colthurst spoke at an inaugural banquet of his hopes that the railway would promote the practical prosperity of the country (McGrath 1952, p. 55). During its heyday, the line became increasingly important for taking commuters and schoolchildren into Cork, while others used it for golf and tourism. It apparently had a very 'holiday' feel to it, since its coaches were made of bamboo and were open to the winds (O'Hegarty 1949, p. 22). The only real setback was in 1898 when there was a decrease in American visitors and fewer first-class tickets were sold; at the same time a rise in potato prices, after a poor crop, left the purchasers of third-class tickets with less disposable income for outings to Blarney (ibid., p. 20).

A little further up the line from Blarney Castle was another local tourist attraction, the Hydropathic Baths built by Dr Barter at St Anne's Hill in Blarney. It too had a station on the Cork & Muskerry Light Railway. Although it is not connected with the castle, it is interesting to note how tourism was developing in different directions in the area. The Hydropathic Baths, of which there were a number throughout the British Isles, were perhaps most like the spas of Europe, although St Anne's was not supplied with its own distinctive mineral water or mud. Dr Barter had discovered that hot, steamy Turkish baths, also known for a while as 'Irish Baths' (Osman, 1988, p. 1) were apparently beneficial for a number of medical conditions. He opened his baths in his large house in 1856 and then, after their increasing success, rebuilt the house to accommodate more guests in 1860. The advertisements for the baths stress the scenic quality of the area; for example, in 1898: 'Fine situation, picturesque scenery.' (Osman, 1988, p. 3)

Effectively the hydro was like a health farm; it boasted fresh food, plain living, massage and recreations such as billiards, a library, cards, tennis, croquet, a putting green, golf at Dripsey and outings to Killarney and, of course, Blarney Castle, all under medical supervision. Its most famous client was probably 'Father Matthew', the temperance campaigner.

The railways continued to flourish until the Civil War, when they became a focus of political and military activity; they were frequently targeted by the Republicans in an effort to undermine the Free State. On the night of 14 August 1922 a large number of road and rail bridges around Blarney were blown up. These included the Monard Viaduct and the Leemount/Carrigrohane Bridge across the Lee, which carried the tracks of the Muskerry Tram. The viaduct was hastily repaired and was back in use in a fortnight, only to be attacked again on 29 September. The Free State was concerned to keep this vital part of Ireland's infrastructure working and created a special force, composed of unemployed railway workers, to repair tracks and other damage (Mulcahy, in prep.). Military posts were established to protect vulnerable spots such as viaducts and this led to a shift in Republican tactics. There were several cases of trains being held up or shot at. The troops guarding the Monard Viaduct were involved in one of the most dramatic incidents in the Blarney area. On 8 November 1922 the Republicans held up the 7.20 am to Mallow and sent an empty engine hurtling at 50 mph towards a stationary train full of Free State troops guarding the viaduct. One of the soldiers, Sergeant O'Leary, was a former railway worker and had the presence of mind to lift the track in front of the troop train so that the runaway train was derailed, preventing it from doing serious damage. The engine fell onto its side and O'Leary prevented an explosion by shutting off the engine's boiler (ibid.).

The damage suffered by the Cork & Muskerry Light Railway had a longer-lasting financial effect on it and the surrounding area. When the Carrigrohane Bridge, which carried the tracks from Cork northwards towards Blarney, was blown up on 14 August the service was cut off. Train services were suspended and most of the 300 employees of the company were laid off. Since many of the road bridges locally had also been lost this resulted in a terrible disruption to transport and local commerce, which particularly affected the farmers (ibid.). For a fortnight there was no service at all; after that there was an emergency passenger-only service which ran to each end of the bridge. Trippers could no longer visit the castle so easily.

On 7 September 1922 the mail train was held up at Leemount (ibid.) and two days later there was a shoot-out at the station which resulted in a Free State soldier and his civilian companion being abducted and an IRA man being mortally wounded.

The limited service run after August 1922 meant that there was no more freight businesses. As a result there was a marked decrease in the company's income, down to £636 in 1922–3, against £3,259 in the previous financial year. The War of Independence depressed many businesses, including tourism, in any case but the disruption and these heavy losses may have contributed to the decline of the service and its ultimate closure.

Although it no longer has a railway service, tourism to Blarney is healthy. It is convenient for Cork Airport, and there is still a ferry service to Ringaskiddy. The castle retains its advantages of being close to a major city centre, but visitors now come by car, bus, or coach. Visitors have not come on the Cork & Muskerry Light Railway since 1934. After the War of Independence and the Civil War it was absorbed into the Southern Railway and then fell victim to competition from the more flexible motor bus. The Great Western & Southern line railway station closed too and is now a private house. The local railway lines, overtaken by the combustion engine, followed the outside jaunting car into extinction. This is most poignantly symbolised by the old station yard at Blarney – the station building still stands amid an expanse of coaches and cars, in what has now become that essential space, the visitors' car park. Some European heritage organisations are trying to encourage visitors to use public transport to visit their properties, and perhaps recent environmental thinking will see tourists reaching Blarney in new ways this century.

CHAPTER 10
A Tour of Blarney Castle

THE CASTLE IS a complex building and it must be remembered that there were two major periods of construction. Firstly a courtyard castle of a familiar European type, with towers at each corner, was built probably between 1480 and 1494. This earlier castle was mostly demolished when the main tower house was built. Fig. 19 shows how the castle would appear if sliced down the middle (and the key at the right) shows the different, approximate, periods of modification. These periods correspond to the rule of certain chieftains (genealogical tables Figs. 3–5). Chapter 11 expands on these changes.

The site and how the valley was formed

Blarney Castle stands in a lush, well-watered valley of meadows. This valley originated in the Ice Age when a glacier scoured it out, forming a prehistoric lake. The western end of this lake eventually drained to the south and cut a steep valley between the hills to meet the River Lee. The Shournagh River now flows down this 'canyon' to the south of the Blarney estate. Mud settled in the trapped waters of the lake to form a bog called the Inchancomain to the east (Hillyard 1959, p. 3), part of which survives, if only in name. The Blarney (Com-abhan or Comeen; 'crooked stream') River drains this ancient bog. Until the seventeenth century water seeped westward through the then-extensive bog, thickly wooded with alder, yew and sessile oak. The Blarney River we see now has been canalised to drain the land and runs between neat banks well below the meadow near the castle.

The tower house stands on a spur of ice-resistant rock north-east of the former marshland at the confluence of the Blarney and the Martin rivers. This site was dry, defensible and offered easy access to the rich food resources of the marshland. It is therefore no surprise to learn that a cave in the rock under the north-west angle of the tower house may have been utilised by man long before the castle was built.

FROM THE CAR PARK TO THE CASTLE

The environment

The visitors' entrance to the estate was once the yard of a railway station built in 1887 (Ch. 9) and closed in 1934. The visitor is confronted, on passing through the modern ticket office, with a handsome well-watered meadow scattered with magnificent trees, which almost hide the castle in the distance. This natural-looking parkland is the result of careful landscaping and reclamation over hundreds of years. The 1936 Ordnance Survey records, to all intents and purposes, the present landscape (Fig. 7b).

The path to the castle at first runs along the north side of the Martin River, crossing at a footbridge where the northernmost channel of the Blarney River meets the Martin. The Blarney has been canalised into three channels (Fig. 7b). These meet the Martin at different bridges that carry the path towards the castle. In the past the shallow Blarney River spread to form a wide stony ford immediately north of the tower house (Fig. 8), where now two narrow channels are bridged by the path.

In exceptional circumstances the valley can still flood: the last time this happened was 1948. On another occasion 'a picturesque bridge [. . .] which led to the castle' depicted by Gordon Holmes in 1797 (Fig. 8) was 'swept away by the wintry floods' (Crofton Croker 1824, p. 305). At about this time the floor of the valley formed an ornamental lake in which the castle could be seen in picturesque reflection. An engraving of 1831 (Fig. 9) recorded its appearance, but this lake seems to have been drained soon after, because it is not shown on the 1841 6 inch Ordnance Survey map.

As the visitor crosses the second bridge the tower comes into view, surrounded by tiers of walls around its base. These walls range in date from the fifteenth to the nineteenth century and reflect the different buildings made at various times, chief of which was the 'mansion house' (Fig. 10), dating probably from the late sixteenth century, which stood in various forms until 1820–21 when it burned down.

As Blarney Castle has never undergone a full archaeological excavation, the best tool for understanding the building at present is the observation of subtle differences in the style of masonry. For example, the Watchkeeper's Tower standing in isolation east of the tower house, next to the southernmost of the three streams, looks as if it could be nineteenth century, its mortar ornamented by chips of stone. It is in fact original; further examination shows that the base of the tower is a different shape from the superstructure and is of rough, unadorned masonry. The ragged stump of a curtain wall can be seen to join it and it must therefore have formed part of a circuit of walls around the tower house.

Describing masonry and architectural features requires a series of specific technical terms to ensure there is no ambiguity about what is meant. A glossary of these terms is provided at the end of the book to avoid encumbering the text with unnecessary repetitive explanation.

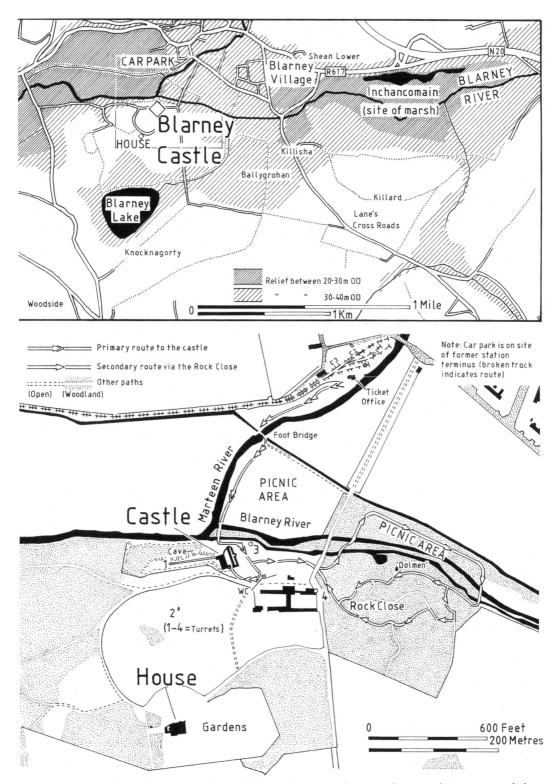

Fig. 7 Blarney Castle and its surroundings a) Physical features of surrounding area b) Recommended route.
[Ordnance Survey of Ireland Permit No. 8372 © Ordnance Survey of Ireland and Government of Ireland]

Fig. 8 View of the tower house from the north-west in 1797, showing the wide ford and the complete parapet. ('Blarney Castle', drawn by Gordon Holmes, 15 September 1797; engraved by J. & H. S. Glover; published by Sherwood & Co., 1 July 1824. Plate to J. Brewer's The Beauties of Ireland.) [National Library of Ireland, Irish Topographical prints and original drawings, 173 TA].

Fig. 9 Distant view of Blarney Castle from the east in the 1830s, showing the freshly ruined mansion reflected in the flooded valley. ('Blarney Castle'; W.H. Bartlett. Thos. Dixon Fisher, Sr., 1831. Plate to G.N. Wright's Ireland Illustrated.) [National Library of Ireland, Irish Topographical prints and original drawings, 174 TA].

Fig. 10 View of Blarney Castle and the mansion from the north-north-east in the 1790s, showing the tower-house roof in situ. ('Blarney Castle', drawn by J. Nixon; engraved by J. Walker; published by Harrison and Co., 1 January 1794. Plate to G. N. Wright's Ireland Illustrated.) [National Library of Ireland, Irish Topographical prints and original drawings, 169 TA]

The 'bawn' (outer enclosures)

The term 'bawn' (*bádhun*) simply means an 'enclosure for cows' but has long been used to describe the outer defences of a Gaelic castle. The Blarney bawn was particularly extensive. John Windele, a nineteenth-century local historian, commented that 'a space of ground [once existed], whose interior area forming the bawn, it is said contained eight acres' (1839, p. 235). It probably comprised two very large oblong enclosures running more or less parallel with the south side of the Blarney River on either side of the tower. Recent examination (Power 1997, pp. 358–60) shows that it was surrounded by a curtain wall. The following section describes the bawn in an anticlockwise circuit starting from the footbridge; unfortunately a number of obstacles mean that this route cannot be followed on the ground, but individual features can be seen at other points during the visit.

After the visitor crosses the last bridge a length of curtain wall can be seen to the right of the north face of the tower (see below). This revetment escaped the general demolition of the curtain walls (probably in the late eighteenth century). The wall runs 64.2 metres (210 feet) west of the tower (Fig. 7). It formed the north wall of the bawn and continues the line of the north face of the tower. It is separated from the castle by a wide gap, thought to have been the result of a collapse (Power 1997, p. 360) but a 1797 view (Fig. 8) shows that the gap was formerly occupied by a building with a mullioned and transomed window. A barrel-vaulted sub-structure yet remains of this building above the quarry.

The curtain wall is 'double skinned': the outer wall is separated from a thin inner wall by a filling of soil and loose stones, part of which has been removed (Fig. 11). The soil formed an inner rampart to absorb the shock of cannonballs. This reinforcement of the castle's defences was probably carried out by the Mac Carthys in the 1640s, shortly before Broghill's siege and may have allowed the rampart to bear cannons. Each merlon of the crow-stepped parapet is perforated by a gunloop for a musket. The Muskerry armoury would have had to be well-stocked to defend all these positions.

The west end of the bawn wall terminates in a two-storey tower, oval in plan, later converted into a dovecote. Each floor of the tower is supplied with five gunloops. The demolished bawn wall would have continued south, to form the west side of the courtyard. This vanished wall probably ran between the dovecote tower and another tower which now stands in isolation (Power 1997, p. 360) within the garden of Blarney House. This second tower formed the south-west corner of the bawn. It stands directly on virgin rock and the scars of the demolished west wall and a vanished southern wall can be seen in its fabric. A third tower stands at the east end of the great stable block of the Victorian house, about 210 metres (689 feet) east-north-east of the second tower and well to the east of the castle itself. The presence of musketloops date these walls and towers to the period after guns became widely available, about 1500.

Fig. 11 Distant view of the west side of the castle with the bawn wall in the foreground.

The quarry and the north face of the castle

The visitor standing on the bridge can see that the north wall of Blarney Castle sits directly on a cliff of rock, formed when stone for the castle was quarried out. The cliff is about 8 metres (25 feet) high and makes the tower house look higher. Crofton Croker recorded:

> Since I am on the subject of discoveries, it may be worth notice that, in a quarry close to the castle, where some men were working, we picked up several human bones, and that one of the labourers informed us so many as twenty horseloads of these bones had been thrown into the lake; he also spoke of two or three spear-heads being found with them. Groats and pennies of the Edwards and Henries have been frequently dug up here; but I believe never in any great quantity. (1824, p. 305)

Some general points about the castle are best appreciated at this point. Close up, the castle seems to diminish with height, due to its vast size. This is an optical illusion, but it *does* in fact get smaller as it gets higher because each wall slopes gently inwards. The west wall slopes (batters) no less than 0.61 metres (2 feet) inwards from the base at 22 metres (72 feet 6 inches) height (Leask 1951, Fig. 78).

A vertical 'seam' or joint in the north wall demonstrates that the castle was built in two stages. Large, neatly-cut quoin stones at the corners show the right-hand portion to be older: a tall thin tower built as an independent structure. The base of the north wall was originally part of an earlier curtain wall built at the same time as the north-west tower and using the same very large blocks of stone, quite distinct from the smaller stones used in the later tower house. There is therefore no 'seam' towards the base. The north-west tower is lower than the taller, later tower house.

The oriel window

The casemented oriel window which projects from the north wall (Fig. 12) is most unusual in Irish castles; it is the window of the room called the Earl's Chamber. This late addition is typical of improvements that made the castle a more tolerable place to live in, and it was also a status symbol. The oriel's date (1515–39) is betrayed by the cyma recta moulding that forms the top of the window. The wall below these windows is made of finished, cut stone (ashlar) bordered by plain-chamfered cornices. The sides are slightly canted, the whole structure being supported by three pyramidal corbels.

Other openings

The treatment of the window heads is varied and no attempt has been made to create a uniform effect. The loops of the tower house are dressed with large chamfered dressings but those in the north-west tower are smaller, narrower and cruder.

The three large square holes which can be seen in the wall (two left of the 'seam' and one near the north-west angle) are the outlets for garderobes in the chambers. It was customary and practical for the garderobes to be placed downwind. The largest opening has a Carmarthen arch over it at first-floor level.

High up, two identical two-light windows can be seen. These are ornamented with ogival arches and hood moulds. They were not glazed, which indicates that they are very early features. They date from the construction of the tower house (Period 2) and are seen in both the old and later work. The tall loop at the base of the tower is a confusing amalgam from several periods (see below).

The walls now are largely bare stone, but evidence of their original colour and finish is suggested in the *Annals of the Four Masters*:

> Cormac, son of Teige, son of Cormac Oge Mac Carthy, Lord of Muskerry, a comely-shaped, bright countenanced man, who possessed most whitewashed

Fig. 12 View from below of the north-west angle, showing the oriel.

85

edifices, fine-built castles, and hereditary seats of any of the descendants of Eoghan Mor. (McCarthy 1922, p. 192)

Blarney, like other tower houses, was coated in a soft, permeable render to prevent the penetration of water. The shaded north wall was particularly susceptible to damp. Patches of hard mortar of various periods still remain on the walls; the renders on the tower house and north-west tower are quite distinct, and the mortar of the later building can be seen slopping around the angle of the north-west tower.

The eighteenth-century occupants hung slates over much of the castle in an attempt to fight damp. The uneven distribution of the slate hints at the past existence of lean-to buildings against the north wall (and suggests that the garderobes were no longer in use).

The north face was capped with a crow-stepped parapet. Now greatly damaged, its original form is shown in Holme's 1797 view (Fig. 8). The different heights of the turret and added tower were exploited to picturesque effect by raising the parapet to a central crow-stepped peak. The same view also shows the lookout point on the north-east angle (top left), now truncated. This point was, until about 1870, the original home of the Blarney Stone.

Three conical, dressed-stone rainwater outlets can be seen near the left summit of the north face. Crude slabs serve this purpose on the older north-west tower. These outlets may seem insignificant but are evidence that the huge machicolations that run around the tower are not original. Rainwater usually passed through holes in the base of the parapet and projecting gutter stones threw this cascade clear of the vulnerable harling. This system did not work at Blarney because the ejected water could not fall clear of the sloping wallface below. This problem was eventually remedied at great effort and expense by building new machicolations (p. 118).

The 'dog kennels'

Turning left from the footbridge, the path to the castle entrance rises gently before swinging around to the right. There is a wall on the right-hand side of the path, pierced by two doorways leading into barrel-vaulted chambers. These are traditionally identified as dog kennels. The path was probably covered by a gatehouse at this point: the footings of a possibly seventeenth-century wall run along the left side of the path above the stream. This perhaps formed the north side of this building.

The first door leads to a small barrel-vaulted chamber with recesses in either side. The presence of sockets and rebates show that the doors of both chambers were fastened internally – any dogs kept here must have shut themselves in at night, a feat few dogs are capable of. It seems more likely that these were guardrooms, given their position in what was probably the gatehouse passage. Whatever their role, the mysterious chambers are later in date than the north-east bastion (see below) because several of its musket-loops were blocked by their construction.

The north-east bastion

The confusing mass of masonry beyond the dog kennels is the base of a sixteenth-century D-shaped bastion that guarded the north-east corner of the tower house and the approach to its entrance. Originally this tower must have formed one of the 'four piles, joined in one, seated upon a main rock, so that it is free from mining. The wall being eighteen feet thick and well flanked at each corner to the best advantage' that was mentioned in the *Pacata Hibernia* (Stafford 1896, p. 227). This bastion encloses a complex of underground passages and chambers dating from different periods, whose sequence of building and layout have yet to be fully unravelled. Various features which are now inaccessible are mentioned in old accounts.

Above the remains of the bastion there is the surviving base of the mansion. The rounded sides of the bastion tower were adapted by corbelling to accommodate the north wall of the house (Fig. 10). The D-shaped north-east tower was altered on several occasions and reused window stones have been noted in the keyhole-shaped gunloops (Power 1997, p. 360). The loops are simple slits with slight widenings to take a gun barrel. Traces of plaster can still be seen on these gunloops.

The modern entrance cuts open the core of the bastion to reveal, in the passage, a doorway raised about 1.7 metres (5 feet 6 inches) above the ground. Through the doorway may be seen a little D-shaped 'first-floor' chamber to one side of the entrance. It is roughly 1.95 metres (6.39 feet) north–south and 4 metres (13 feet) east–west within the north part of the tower. Three keyhole-shaped loops or small windows (now blocked) enfiladed the ground west of the tower but are now blocked by the 'kennels'.

On the east (left) side of the modern entrance passage is a very small room with a vaulted ceiling which has a single loop. Although the interior of the bastion is traditionally identified as a prison (see below), there is no evidence of any timber doors.

Further inside the bastion two parallel stairs ascend from the outside, separated by a thick wall of masonry. There is evidence for a partially blocked connecting passage between the two stairs. The right-hand (west) stair's ceiling is neatly roofed with rectangular slabs fitted edge to edge but elsewhere the ceilings are crudely corbelled. The stair inexplicably climbs a short height to a blocked ceiling, a reminder of the complex development of this building. The left-hand (east) stair is significantly cruder in construction and must be climbed with care; another well-preserved blocked loop can be seen in its side.

The chambers at the top of the stairs are terraced into the side of the rock. The staircase gives onto a painfully low passage leading into an irregular roundish chamber about 1.25 metres (4.1 feet) north–south and 1.9 metres (6.25 feet) east–west with a corbelled ceiling. An extremely deep embrasure in the west side of the room gives onto a gunloop, again externally blocked. This chamber probably housed a well, now filled in. An early account of Blarney Castle describes a 'well and prison' which were approached by 'an open (*sic*) in the solid rock' at the north-east corner of the tower house (Windele 1839, p. 235).

An irregular tunnel burrows gently downwards and to the left from the round chamber, apparently under the foundations of the tower house. It ends in a small cave in the virgin rock 16.5 metres (54 feet 1 inch) from the chamber but this can only be approached on one's stomach and is not part of the recommended itinerary of the castle! Broghill's siege in 1646 (Cruise O'Brien 1972, p. 54) may have led to the excavation of this tunnel as part of an attempt to undermine the castle. The attempt was apparently abandoned when the castle surrendered. According to Windele's account, further stairs and passages were supposed to exist, including one to the tower house; these seem to have been blocked up over the centuries and their sites forgotten.

The Court

Continuing up the path to the entrance, the remains of the eighteenth-century mansion house or 'Court' can be seen. Only the foot of the east wall, draped with creepers, to one side of the sloping footpath remains (Fig. 14). This is the ruin of the Gothick house rebuilt by James St John Jefferyes to the east of the tower house after he inherited the property in 1739. It was damaged by fire in 1820 or 1821 and the fixtures and building materials were then sold off by auction (MacCarthy 1990, p. 163). This may explain the rumour recorded by Fitzgerald, the self-styled 'Bard of the Lee', that the 'Court' was deliberately dismantled by James St John Jeffereys to prevent his son from inheriting it (1899, p. 19).

The northern part of the house was given a basement to accommodate the rockface (see above) and only the lowest courses of the basement windows survive. Old views and photographs show that the house was three storeys high with ranges of casemented windows facing east (Fig. 10). In 1838 a Dublin artist nostalgically reminisced on life in the house under the formidable Arabella Jefferyes in the first years of the nineteenth century, 'a patroness of the highest class in society, and of the most spirited and generous disposition' (Notes and Queries, 1895, p. 82, see also Ch. 8).

The southern part of the house appears to be earlier. There is a 'kiosk' (Fig. 14) at the midpoint of the ruin's east wall, behind which is a quoined angle that may indicate the house's original north-east corner. The house was ornamented with elaborate ogival parapets, crenellated to imitate the tower house behind.

The eastern exterior wall

Up the path the visitor has a good view of the vast east wall of the castle (Fig. 15). The masonry is largely obscured by mortar. All the windows seem of a late period but have many minor differences, suggesting different dates of origin.

There are six superficially identical two-light windows, which on closer examination are all seen to be different. All are insertions, because their hood moulds and mullions are stylistically

Fig. 13 General view of the east side of Blarney Castle and the ruins of the mansion before 1977 (after de Breffny 1977). [Photo: George Mott © Thames & Hudson Ltd., London. From Castles of Ireland *by Brian de Breffney, Thames & Hudson Ltd., London]*

Elizabethan (the latter part of the sixteenth century). The first-floor windows are probably pastiche work of eighteenth-century date.

The naked eye can spot some of the subtle clues that reveal changes in the fabric: slight variations in texture or colour. The right-hand window is contemporary with the machicolation but the left window is earlier and is therefore forced into the side of one corbel (Fig. 15). The

Fig. 14 General view of the castle and the kiosk.

machicolation can be dated by such clues. Documentary evidence points to one particular individual as the instigator of these challenging alterations (Ch. 11). Those with really excellent eyesight or binoculars will spot tiny details such as rounded rather than square corners used in one window, but the windows are broadly contemporary.

The south wall and the Blarney Stone

From this point the series of sketch plans (Figs. 20ff.) will help to explain the complexities of the layout. Past the gatehouse the south and west walls of the castle can be seen. At the base of the south wall there is a low truncated wall covered with the stumps of ancient yews. It seems to mark the site of an outbuilding. The ruin and the yew trees may explain the lack of comment in the past on a very interesting feature that can now be seen clearly. The south wall is not straight. Instead, a corner of an earlier building projects on the right-hand side (Fig. 16). This is very probably a corner of the earlier courtyard castle (Period 1) of which the north-west tower formed part. This original south wall can be traced for 5.1 metres (16 feet 5 inches). It is massive and has a pronounced batter on both observable faces, which suggests it is the counterpart of the north-west tower (Ch. 11) rather than a curtain wall.

To the right of the base, a glacis below two gunloops eliminates a deadspot (Fig. 17). The glacis was built after the construction of the gatehouse (see below).

There is a large iron-barred window at first-floor level, punched through in the eighteenth century and removing almost all trace of any earlier openings; two similar windows can be seen on the west wall. These holes allowed timber casement windows (the bars are modern).

Further up the multiple-light south windows are enlargements of earlier windows and are late sixteenth century, like those of the east wall. The second- and fourth-floor original sills (Period 2) can be seen in the wall below the Period 4 openings. The second-floor window presumably resembled the surviving twin-light ogival window in the north wall. The fourth-floor window had a single light (Fig. 18). Perhaps the old windows were the source of the

Fig. 15 The upper part of the east wall of the tower house.

window parts reused in the bastion.

The Blarney Stone can be seen from below here. The stone is the lintel between the third and fourth corbels. The iron straps were possibly added to counteract damage caused by souvenir hunters.

The west wall and north-west tower

The tower house was built on a level foundation platform of rough stones and mortar, which is partially exposed on this face. It is not parallel with the superstructure (Fig. 19). Such minor adjustments in alignment are evident throughout the Period 2 tower house. The contrast between the rough construction of the base of the tower house and the neater masonry of the earlier tower is immediately apparent.

The observable displacement to the west of the south windows of the north-west tower may seem a minor point but could indicate that a curtain wall joined the south side of the north-west tower. Only one floor retains its original single-light windows; the rest have all been modified at least once.

Sunlight on the southern battlement casts the stonemasons' tooling into sharp relief. The faces of the corbels are punched, while the arrises are drafted with a pitcher. The machicolation on the north-west tower is separated by a slight gap from the wall of the tower house. It stops rather suddenly on the west wall of the north-west tower (Fig. 30); the reason for this is conjectured later in the tour.

Fig. 16 Base of possible early tower embedded in south wall.

The gatehouse

Returning to the entrance, the gatehouse runs into the south-east corner of the tower house and projects in an east-south-east direction. It is 16.1 metres (53 feet) long (Power 1997, p. 359) and is more akin to a thick wall than a building. The lost, sharply pitched roof met the south-east corner of the tower house. Quoins were removed from the corner and the edge of the roof was built tucked under the break, resulting in the survival of a fragment of the slated roof. A hidden modern roof now keeps the building dry.

The gate is an unusual essay in the Renaissance style, rarely used by Gaelic chieftains (Fig. 21). The round arch with a dropped keystone is covered by a square hood with stepped label stops. A hole in the east jamb held the securing chain for the yett (grille) of 'intricately fashioned iron bars' (Hillyard 1959, p. 5). The gate and yett caught the eye of an early vicar of Blarney, who installed them in his glebe house. They were carefully restored by a member of the Royal Society of Antiquaries of Ireland in the late nineteenth century and can be still seen in situ (Fig. 21).

A 'grate' is mentioned in Cormac Mac Teige's will of 1583 (Gillman 1892b, p. 197). Mention of a grate would place the gatehouse before 1583, but this may refer to an earlier *yett* on the tower house itself (p. 99).

Entering the gate, the visitor can see how the gatehouse's upper storey was originally reached by a narrow and now fragmentary spiral stair to the right of the entrance passage. The first-floor chamber would have been a good defensive site, since it overlooks the surrounding area through gunloops in the west end and the north wall, with an additional opening in the eastern 'tip'. The barred south opening over the gate marks the site of an earlier window.

The gatehouse also functioned as a bastion. Its layout permitted raking fire along the south and east walls of the tower house. Such a sophisticated defensive feature was no doubt added at a later date. The stump of the south wall of the later mansion is appended to the southern 'tip'.

The 'oubliette'

In the nineteenth century one of the castle's most lurid attractions was the so-called 'oubliette', a hole in which prisoners were put, below floor level, to be 'forgotten'. This hole was sited in front of the main entrance. It is now

Fig. 7 Glacis between the gatehouse and the south wall.

well hidden and inaccessible but was supposedly once reached by another passage, now blocked up. It is a conical pit allegedly 15.24 metres (50 feet) deep, opening in the ground in front of the main entrance to the tower house. Its operation was fancifully described by Mary Hillyard in 1959 as follows:

> [L]et into its cone-shaped ceiling is a large paving stone which lies in front of the main keep doorway. By an ingenious arrangement, the gate keeper could upon instructions welcome in a visitor, loose a catch upon a wall, and as the victim stepped forward, the stone would turn over and the ground swallow him up. (p. 4)

At the risk of spoiling a good story, it is possible that the pit served as a granary.

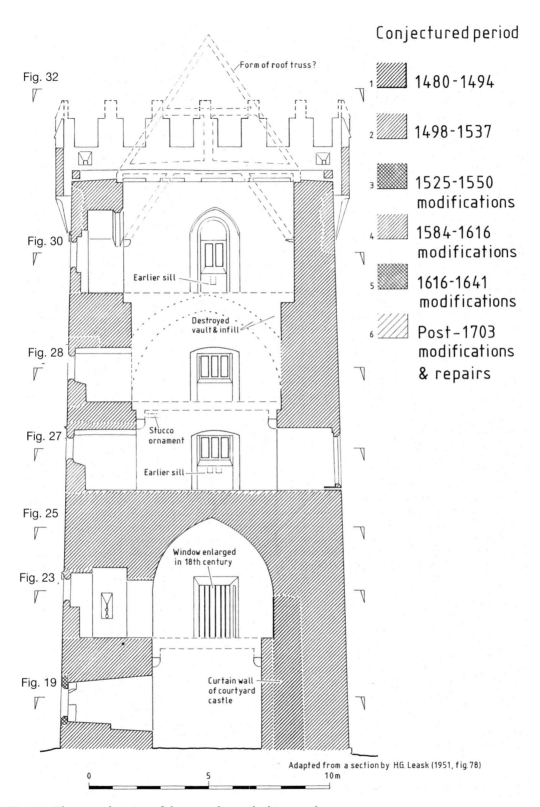

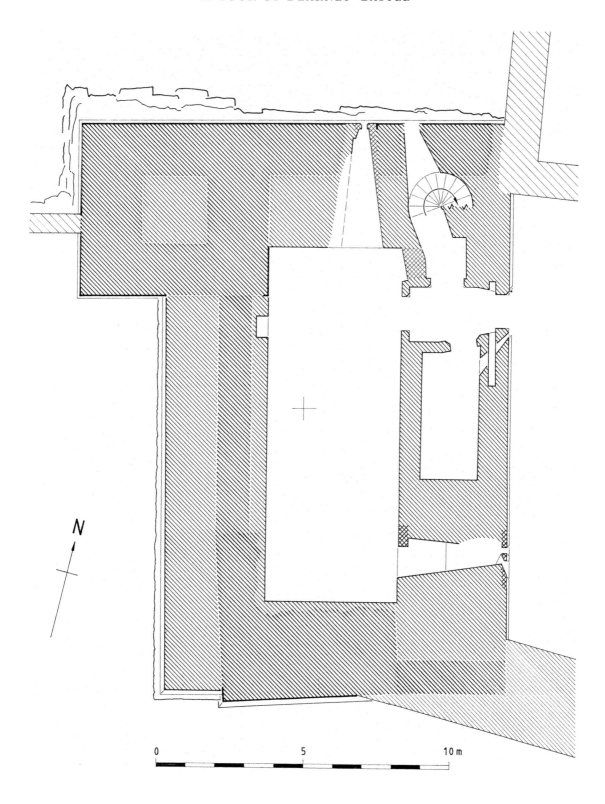

Fig. 19 Plan of the ground floor of the tower and the tower house. Dark hatchings show the courtyard castle.

Fig. 20 Detail of the west wall of the tower house and the south wall of the north-west tower

THE INTERIOR OF THE CASTLE

Tower ground floor

The modern visitor's route through the castle reverses the order in which the chambers were approached in the seventeenth century. Beginning at the most private and heavily defended areas of the building, the rest of the visit involves working one's way out again through the original entrance route.

The original Period 2 doorways of the tower house are distinguished by their stone dressings: pointed arches, chamfers and chamfer stops at the base. Later doors in contrast are simply punched through the walls and lack these fine dressings. All original doors in the tower house opened inwards, away from the visitor, and could be locked and barred with lengths of timber to protect those inside, but these timber doors have long since been removed.

The main entrance and 'lobby'

The castle doorway (Fig. 22) is seen to the left (beyond the shop). The massive entrance is sunk into a recess and is dressed with hard Cork Limestone, capable of resisting the largest crowbars and hammers. Windows, doors and other features were all dressed from this hard marble-like stone which is very resistant to weathering.

For additional security, the studded timber door was protected by another hinged iron yett, now gone. The vanished yett swung on two large iron pintles; one of which points downwards (Fig. 22). The other (missing) pintle would have pointed upwards to prevent the yett from being lifted off its hinges. A fastening chain through the hole in the left-hand rebate was secured in the large guard chamber beyond (inaccessible). When empty, this hole acted as a speaking tube between the guard and visitors and also as a gunloop to deal with undesirables.

The timber door behind the yett was probably of two-ply oak and studded with nail heads in

Fig. 21 The Renaissance Gate.

patterns. The door was further reinforced by a large drawbeam: a beam of timber that normally slid out of sight in a socket in the south side. A conventional lock and key was probably also employed but no sign of these remains. If attackers broke through the main entrance and into the lobby, they could be despatched from above through the murder hole (now blocked; see below) in the vaulted ceiling.

Traditionally, keeping your gate open to all comers (especially bards in search of hospitality) was the noble attribute most likely to be praised in verse. When the chieftain was in residence the door normally lay open, but no visitor escaped the surveillance of the hereditary Mac Sweeney gallowglas guard. This was where Donell McOyn illoyghey (an locha), the Mac Sweeney mentioned in Cormac Mac Teige's 1583 will, would have sat, waiting to question visitors (Gillman 1892b, p. 197).

Even representatives of enemy forces could expect liquid refreshment as their due: in 1602 the English tried to exploit this inviolable custom to capture the castle by guile. They did not understand that the open-door policy only applied when the chieftain was at home. The Mac Carthy chieftain, Cormac Mac Dermot Mor was at that time enjoying English hospitality in a Cork prison (Ch. 7).

There are two categories of room in the tower house: large and small, the latter being built within the thickness of the walls. The east wall of the tower house is 3.78 metres (12.4 feet) thick and easily contains the entrance lobby and guardroom. The entrance to the dark ground-floor chamber was left open, but a heavy timber door closed off the main spiral stair. Both the outer and inner doors of the lobby are 1.1 metres (3.6 feet) wide, much wider than the other doors in the tower house. In West Cork tower houses the basement had no communication with the rest of the building; this may indicate it was used as a temporary refuge for farm animals (Samuel 1998, p. 77). However, there is no suggestion that the probably vast Mac Carthy Muskerry herds were accommodated in Blarney's basement.

The basement chamber

The modern visitor should disregard the spiral stair and enter the basement. The room seems to be of a tremendous height, but the barrel vault that can be seen is in fact the ceiling of the first-floor chamber. The walls bear many rough coats of plaster and the extremely uneven ground floor is divided by a step into two levels.

The room was originally divided horizontally with a ponderously carpentered ceiling, which formed the floor of the first-floor chamber. Two long beams (wall plates) ran down the length of the room, resting on the rows of massive corbels in the east and west walls. Lighter joists ran across the width, supported by the wall plates (Fig. 18). Floorboards were then placed on top, running lengthways. The door and window embrasures now give onto only air at first-floor level. Three of the largest chambers of the tower house are now floorless and so can only be inspected from a distance. Fortunately all the stairs are of stone.

It has long been assumed that the basement was some sort of storeroom. A thousand barrels of wheat were stored at Barnahely Castle (East Cork) in 1642 (Power 1994, p. 221). Presuming that cattle were not kept here, it is more likely to have been used for dry goods and perhaps beer, mead and imported wine (Samuel 1998, p. 117). It is possible that Blarney's basement functioned as a buttery where French wine was decanted from barrels. An anecdote about another Mac Carthy chieftain at the Castle of Togher relates that so great was his hospitality that he had casks of Spanish wine poured into the River Bandon to improve the water for his thirsty kerns (McCarthy 1922, p. 134). There would have been a supply of spirits somewhere in the castle: the English who attempted to take the castle by deception in 1602 called for a refreshing morning drink of 'wine and *usquebagh* (whiskey), whereof Irish gentlemen are seldom unfurnished' (Stafford 1896, p. 227).

The dim light in the basement chamber comes through loops in the

Fig. 22 Main entrance.

north and east walls. The north loop originated as an arrow slit in the early curtain wall; its east jamb of roughly split stones survives. The west jamb was later knocked out. Stones from another two-light ogival window were re-employed to make a wider opening. It is probable that at the same time the west side of the embrasure was quarried out, leaving part of the old work in place overhead. These re-employed stones probably came from one of the enlarged windows in the upper floors.

A fine round-headed loop pierces the east wall of the chamber. This and its flanking gunloop were probably inserted in Period 3 (1525–1550, Fig. 18). A hollow was cut in the side of the embrasure to provide clearance for the gunner. The embrasure opening is narrowed to no apparent purpose by a stub wall within. This *may* have formed a hiding place for a defender.

A blocked doorway can be seen near the north-east corner left of the chamber entrance. This is a reminder that provisions had to be carried up the spiral stairs from the basement, a back-breaking chore. A short passage connected the chamber to the foot of the main spiral stair but was later filled in because it posed a threat to security. The work of servants at other Cork tower houses, such as the early and important Kilgobbin Castle near Kinsale, was reduced by the provision of an internal chute through the barrel vault, which allowed heavy items to be hoisted into the upper chambers (Samuel 1998, p. 77). The remains of modern ovens can be seen at the north end of the chamber.

The first-floor chamber

The visitor now climbs a modern timber stair (not shown on plan) that leads to the Earl's Chamber (Fig. 22). This allows closer examination of the remains of the first-floor chamber, a chamber both longer and wider than the room below with great offsets (ledges) in the north and west walls. It is likely that the west wall of the chamber is essentially the original west curtain wall of the enclosure castle (Period 1). The builders of the tower house built a 'thickening' against its east face to provide secure support for the corbels (Fig. 18).

The vaulted ceiling of the first-floor chamber would have been built in the traditional manner. This method of construction is seen throughout Ireland and seems to be an indigenous development. A framework of timber (centring) was first built in the rough shape of the vault. To create the exact curve the builders laid a series of wicker hurdles over the framework which they stiched together at the edges to create a single shell with the exact shape of the vault. It would then be covered in mortar, locking it in place. The timber centring would then be removed and the wickerwork could be plastered over, as here, or left to form a decorative finish. Here a negative cast of the wickerwork centring can be seen where the plaster has fallen away.

This chamber was perhaps originally used as a storeroom but it was eventually made habitable. In the seventeenth century a fine stone fireplace (Fig. 23) was built during the middle of the eastern wall, probably in the chieftainship of the seventeenth Mac Carthy Lord, Cormac Oge (Fig. 19, Period 5). A similar 'Jacobean' fireplace in another Cork tower house, Monkstown

Castle, is dated to 1636 (Power 1997, p. 359). A smaller fireplace was eventually built inside the generous opening of the earlier fireplace in the eighteenth century (Period 6). The very large windows, now barred to deter nesting birds, were probably enlarged in two or three stages. Square-hooded windows were replaced with probably eighteenth century timber-framed windows. These alterations prove the castle was still floored and habitable at a later date than is generally appreciated.

Two inaccessible intramural rooms open off the large chamber (Fig. 24). The small closet to the right of the south window probably held a 'close stool' (a portable box containing a chamber pot) for those being entertained in this chamber.

The east wall contains an intramural passage not accessible to the visitor. Its mullioned window overlooking the forecourt may be a nineteenth-century reconstruction. The south end of the passage gives access to a gunloop (Period 3) with paired holes connected by a vertical sighting slit. This south-east chamber may have continued northwards to the spiral stair before the insertion of the seventeenth-century fireplace. The existing south-east door apparently replaces a blocked door with neat stone dressings immediately to the left of it (Fig. 25). This may have been the main entrance into the first-floor chamber *before* the insertion of the fireplace. If this interpretation is correct, a third door (no more than a rough hole) near the main spiral stair must be seen as the Period 2 door's replacement and the third in sequence.

The north-west tower and Earl's Chamber

The modern timber stair leads into the first storey of the north-west tower (Period 1), known as the Earl's Chamber. In the tower barrel vaults alternated with timber floors as a precaution against fire. Simple central loops in each wall are dressed with limestone and the splayed embrasures have flat stone lintels and bases, slightly raised to serve as seats. There is much variety in size and in the treatment of the window heads.

The Earl's Chamber is entered through a doorway and passage at the head of the timber stair. A heavy modern repair in brick obscures this area but a passage may have existed here since the early sixteenth century. The first reference to this barrel-vaulted room as the Earl's Chamber was in 1839.

> It is accessible with difficulty from within. It is a small arched room, well lit, the floor tiles, and the shreds of tapestry, yet discernable, shew it to have been a chosen apartment; adjoining it is a small closet or anteroom about twelve feet long. (Windele, p. 235)

The south wall displays three small defensive loops, 'square', 'keyhole' and irregular. The first occupies an early window embrasure. An additional embrasure was quarried to the west of it to accommodate the other gunloops. In the west wall there is a large opening of uncertain date above the blocked west loop which, it has been suggested, was an outlet for a fireplace (Crawford Woods 1896, p. 340). It is cut into the blocked remains of a central chamfered loop; its sill is pierced by a slop stone. This feature occurs in some but not all of the original windows of the Period 1 and 2 building campaigns and may have served as a urinal.

The oriel window of fine-cut stone transformed the chamber in the sixteenth century (Ch. 11). The internal timber lintels over the embrasure are conceivably original; scientific dating techniques could determine this.

As part of the first Blarney Castle this room would have been the first storey of the north-west tower (Period 1). It has been partitioned, and the original main entrance to the tower is behind the east (left-hand) wall. That is now blocked; Crawford Woods estimated it to be about 3 metres (10 feet) above the original external ground level (1896, p. 340). Beyond this in the north-east corner is the cramped Black Stairs (Fig. 23).

A bedhead may have stood against the partition (Crawford Woods 1896, p. 340). The tiled floor and 'shreds of tapestry' mentioned by Windele (and now vanished) indicate the special status this room held in later days. Tapestries would have been the most valuable single items in the castle, as is shown from an inventory of a castle made by a plantation settler in Kerry (O'Shea 1983, p. 39). It was probably not an exclusively male domain; a simple curtain could convert the oriel into a small well-lit chamber suitable for the lady of the house and her retinue. It has been suggested that the partial blocking and ragged enlargement of the west opening may mark the site of a makeshift chimney (Crawford Woods 1896, p. 340).

The Black Stairs

The visitor now passes through the narrow doorway in the east wall and turns northwards to the Black Stairs, whose entry is lit by an eighteenth-century brick window. The antiquarian Windele remarked that this staircase could never have 'been intended as a mode of access by any O or Mac who had attained obesity' (1839, p. 235). Nevertheless, it was the original staircase for the north-west tower. After the tower house (Period 2) had been built it was probably no more than a backstairs for servants, it is now the major access route for visitors.

A peculiar recess in the wall on one's right hand (when facing the window) marks the original raised entrance into the north-west tower. The stair is lit by small crude slits, several of which were blocked by the building of the later tower house (Crawford Woods 1896, p. 340), ruling out any possibility that the two are contemporary. A descending curved stair connects the spiral stair to a passage in the north wall of the tower house. This is the 'proper' means of access to the Earl's Chamber and is more easily inspected on the way out of the tower house (p. 129).

About twelve steps up, a small passage runs off to the left to a garderobe in the north wall of the north-west tower. When the oriel's roof was built it blocked the loop that lit the passage. The east jamb of this window can still be seen from outside (Fig. 12).

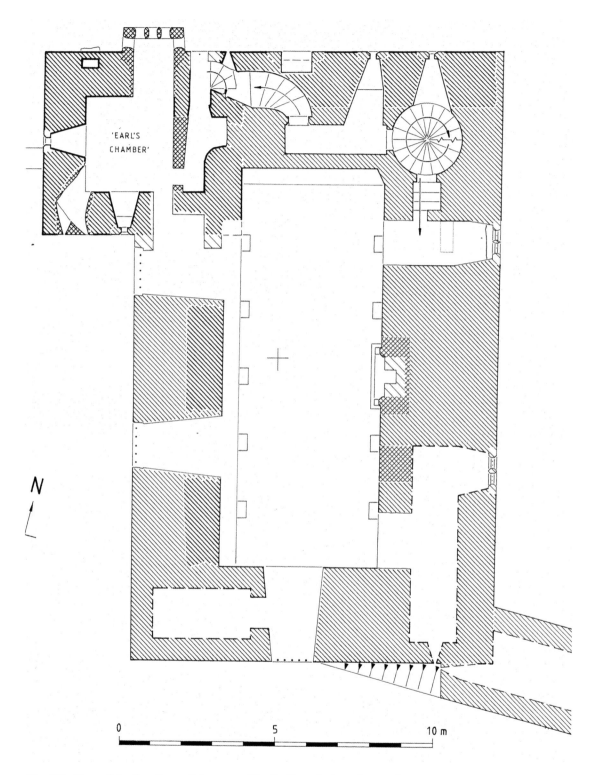

Fig. 23 Plan of the first floor of the tower (Earl's Chamber) and tower house.

Fig. 24 View of the east side of the first-floor chamber, showing fireplace.

The second storey of the north-west tower (The Young Ladies' Chamber)

This chamber is intermediate in level between the first and second floors of the tower house and is entered from the Black Stairs (Fig. 25) through a small door arched by two curved blocks. It is little altered from its fifteenth-century state.

The central ridge on the floor is formed by the apex of the stone vault below and can trip the unwary. A floor on a bed of mortar would have covered the vault originally. The spiral stair projects as a curved housing into the chamber. The three loops have chamfered dressings with ogival or square heads. Internal timber shutters rather than glass were used. Traces of render survive on the wall and two baulks probably of oak form the bases of the west and north window embrasures. These benches of timber also acted as lacing (reinforcement) of the structure. Dendrochronological dating for the tower could be provided using these. The south-west corner is quarried away to create a gunloop at the angle. This too has been identified as a possible fireplace (Crawford Woods 1896, p. 340). The east embrasure shows one of the blockings first noted by Crawford Woods.

The second floor of the tower house is reached through a passage driven through the south-east corner. The visitor should at this stage content themselves with walking down the three steps to a spacious corridor 5.47 metres (18 feet) long. This passage is in the spandrel of the vault and has a curved ceiling. The east (internal) side forms an irregular, thickly rendered mass of brick and

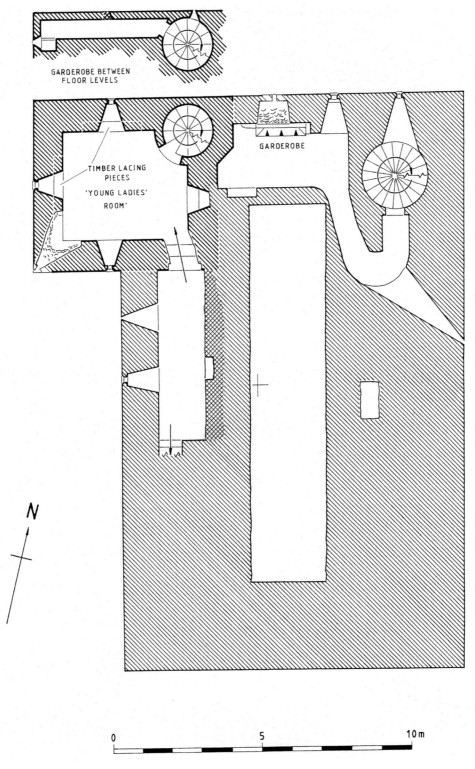

Fig. 25 Plan of the tower house at first-floor mezzanine showing the Young Ladies' Room, the tower garderobe (Period 1) and tower-house garderobe (Period 2).

rubble (Period 6) supporting the arched ceiling, suggesting that the passage was widened in the eighteenth century. A recess is built into this irregular surface. In contrast, the outer (west) wall of the passage is neatly built (Period 2). The impression of a timber-framed door into the chamber probably marks the site of an early stone-arched door.

The traditional identification of this chamber is attractive. Certainly daughters had to be accommodated somewhere; the three young daughters of the fourteenth Lord, Cormac Teige Mac Carthy, are known to have lived at Blarney. Were they accommodated here? Windele, in the earliest specific description of the castle (1839), makes no mention of 'young ladies'. Perhaps an inventive guide subsequently coined the name to give Victorian female visitors a shudder at its almost dungeon-like appearance. The probability is that before 1650 there was a more comfortable house outside the tower house (MacCarthy 1990, p. 164), a precursor to the mid-eighteenth-century mansion.

The third storey of the north-west tower (the Priest's Chamber)

Standing in the Young Ladies' Chamber it is possible to see the next chamber, now floorless, overhead. Corbels projecting from the south and north walls mark the floor. This chamber shares the dimensions of the room below and is covered by a barrel vault; the walls are thickly plastered (Fig. 26). As in the chamber below, the housing of the spiral stair occupies much of the north-east corner, from where the chamber was entered (Fig. 28).

The east window was blocked by the later tower house, but the west window has an unusual round head. It was originally as tall as the other main openings of the tower, although later partially blocked and hidden under the slate hanging. The stones of the ogival south window appear to be shifted from another position. This alone may account for its unusual short shape, but another explanation is possible.

Specific mention of a Priest's Chamber does not apparently exist until the twentieth century; Windele makes no mention of it. Crawford Woods was presumably aware of the tradition when he identified the chamber as the private chapel of the castle (1896, p. 342), but he makes no explicit reference to it.

Comparison with other castles shows that there may well have been a chapel here. One can only speculate that religious iconography, such as wall paintings, survived into the eighteenth century, and it is worth noting that no gunloops were inserted.

In this case, the west window *could* have served as the setting for a small altar while the south opening held a piscina. This would be liturgically incorrect, but such niceties were not always observed in medieval times. It can be compared to a very similar chamber at Kilcoe Castle, which until recently had a partial blocking of the east light with signs of fastenings in the embrasure (Samuel 1998, p. 437); this has a stronger case for identification as a chapel.

Continuing upwards, care is required: the spiral stair between the two chambers climbs at the steep rate of twelve treads in each turn. A narrow opening or squint appears on the right. This connects with a vaulted intramural chamber in the north tower house (Fig. 27). The squint does not permit a direct view into the room but could have been used for communication with the Baroness's Chamber.

The fourth storey of the north-west tower (the 'kitchen')

The highest chamber in the north-west tower is greatly altered from its original form. It must have once closely resembled the Young Ladies' Chamber, though the housing for the spiral stair takes up even more space. A chamfered internal cornice widens the tops of the walls to support the roof timbers. The roof was originally hipped or pyramidal and may have housed a louvre for smoke to escape from a fire below. When first built the chamber probably had four small simple windows, like the surviving west square-headed opening (Period 1).

The first alterations occurred when the tower house was built (Period 2). The east wall was removed to create a broad ascending stair into the highest chamber of the tower house (fourth floor); this runs over the embedded and blocked base of an original east window in the tower (Fig. 28). At the same time, a twin-light window was inserted in the north wall. This handsome window is identical to the north window of the tower house nearby. Both have ogival heads below a rectilinear hood mould. The southern single-light window is unusually wide, tall and has a fine ogival head. It was probably enlarged at the same time. The alterations to the windows suggest that this chamber was uprated to the equivalent of a solar, a feature of English halls. It perhaps formed a separate bedchamber for the tenth Lord, Cormac Oge, and his wife, Catherine Barry, after the completion of the tower house in the early sixteenth century.

The room was effectively cut in half when the west part of the chamber was made into a gigantic fireplace (Period 4) as part of a series of alterations made to the tower house. Standing in the interior of this fireplace looking up, the visitor can see that the width of the enormous chimney decreases with height. The top of the chimney is very unusual, being streamlined from the north rather like a ship's funnel, with a small opening facing south. The two windows were apparently blocked during the era when the fireplace was in use. The chimney breast was supported on a flat arch of joggled (stepped) blocks.

The long cornice running the length of the room on either side and supporting the roof timbers was cut through when the new corbels to support the chimney breast were cut into the wall (Fig. 29). The north corbel half-blocked the window embrasure. Windele's account implies that only the north window was left partially unblocked (1839, p. 235). These blockings have since been removed, except at the base of the southern window.

The fireplace corbels reflect the great corbelled machicolations on the exterior of the tower house, and a joggled flat arch was also used in an inserted second-floor fireplace (see below). All formed part of a series of major alterations to the tower (Period 4) that probably date to the chieftainship of Cormac Mac Dermot Mor Mac Carthy.

A much cruder inserted fireplace breast can be seen on the south side of the chamber. This

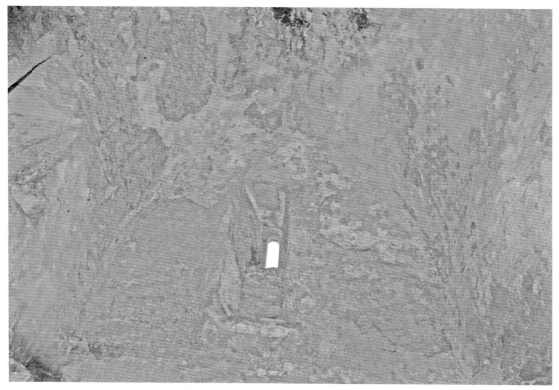

Fig. 26 The west side of the possible chapel (Priest's Chamber), showing plaster.

was cut into the breast of the main fireplace. One twentieth-century guidebook helpfully explains that the sole purpose of the fireplace was to 'heat cauldrons of tar and oil used in defence of the tower house in time of siege' (Hillyard 1959, p. 6). This smacks of the 'Hollywood' interpretation of tower houses. Windele rightly commented that 'a whole animal' could be cooked on a spit in the larger of the two fireplaces and identified the room as a kitchen (1839, p. 235), which seems more plausible. If it is accepted that this chamber was a kitchen it seems certain that the adjoining room served as a dining chamber throughout its history, although the later 'upgrading' of the chambers on lower floors reduced its relative importance (see below).

The wallwalk of the north-west tower

The remainder of the castle (including the Blarney Stone) is presently reached from the top of the Black Stairs. A lintelled doorway allows the visitor to step blinking into the light of day on the wallwalk of the north-west tower. This wallwalk is paved with Cork limestone, finely polished by hundreds of years of use. A lower layer of slabs forms channels between spaced raised slabs (Fig. 30). Both layers slope outwards to funnel rainwater through openings in the base of the parapet and onto rough slabs that project from the wall ('valley system'). The deficiencies of this wallwalk were overcome by the introduction of several refinements on the Period 2 tower house.

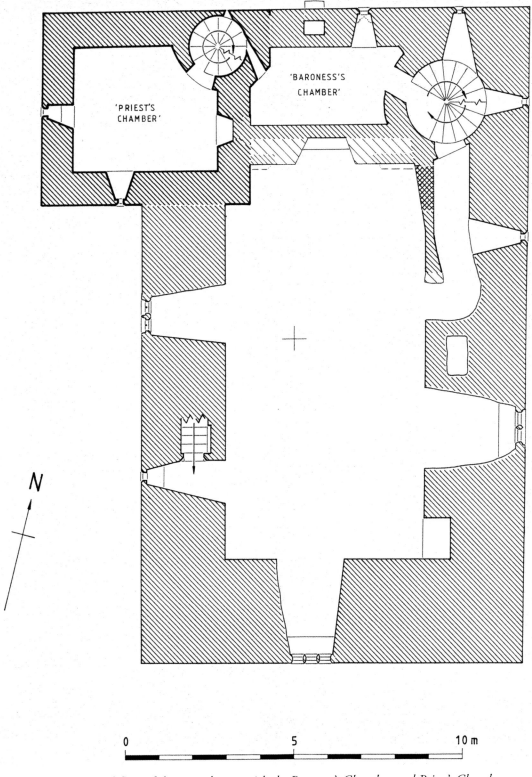

'PRIEST'S CHAMBER'

'BARONESS'S CHAMBER'

N

0   5   10 m

Fig. 27 Plan of second floor of the tower house, with the Baroness's Chamber and Priest's Chamber.

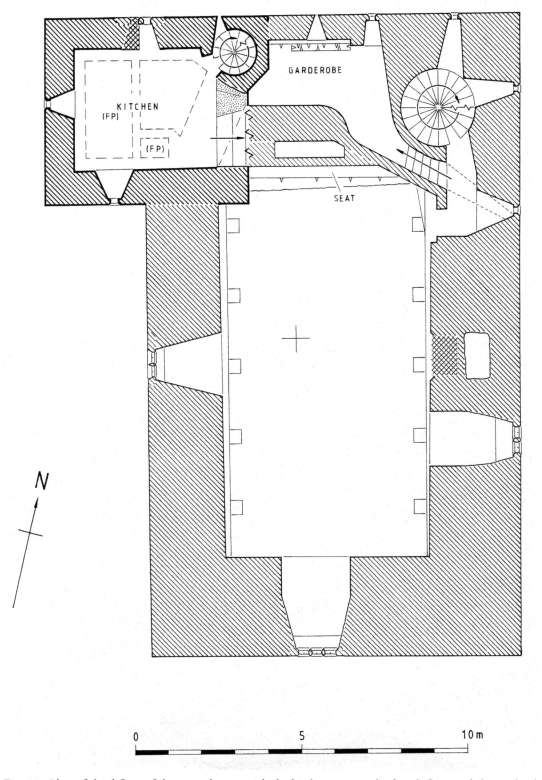

KITCHEN
(FP)

(FP)

GARDEROBE

SEAT

N

0   5   10 m

Fig. 28 Plan of third floor of the tower house, with the kitchen serving the fourth floor and the garderobe chamber.

The north parapet, unlike the wallwalk, was rebuilt as part of the tower house (Period 2) to replace the original parapet of the north-west tower. Old views (e.g., Fig. 8) show an intact parapet descending from the tower house to the north-west tower in a series of crow steps.

On walking around the kitchen 'funnel', the visitor encounters the inside of the elaborate machicolation (Period 4) that clasps the south-west angle (Fig. 20). This aborted machicolation is certainly contemporary though not contiguous with the main tower-house machicolation. The gigantic corbels of the tower-house machicolation can be seen up close at this point (Fig. 31). It appears that the builders wished to run the massive corbelled machiolations all the way round the north side of the tower house but the attempt was probably abandoned for structural reasons, and it was only completed on the south side of the north-west tower.

A stone stair runs from the east end of the south wallwalk to give access to the raised wallwalk of the tower house. This addition (Power 1997, p. 358) is a modern aid to visitors; no sign of it is visible in the 1797 view (Fig. 8) and it appears that there was no circulation between the two levels when the tower house was inhabited. The stair is reached through a gap in the parapet that has clearly been cut through it.

The changes introduced by the building of the tower house were not straightforward. It required the complete removal of the east wallwalk and the upper part of the east wall of the earlier building. A 'bridge' (Fig. 32) was then built to carry the wallwalk of the tower house diagonally over the head of the Black Stairs, leaving the stair housing intact but encased in the

Fig. 29 The kitchen in the north-west tower.

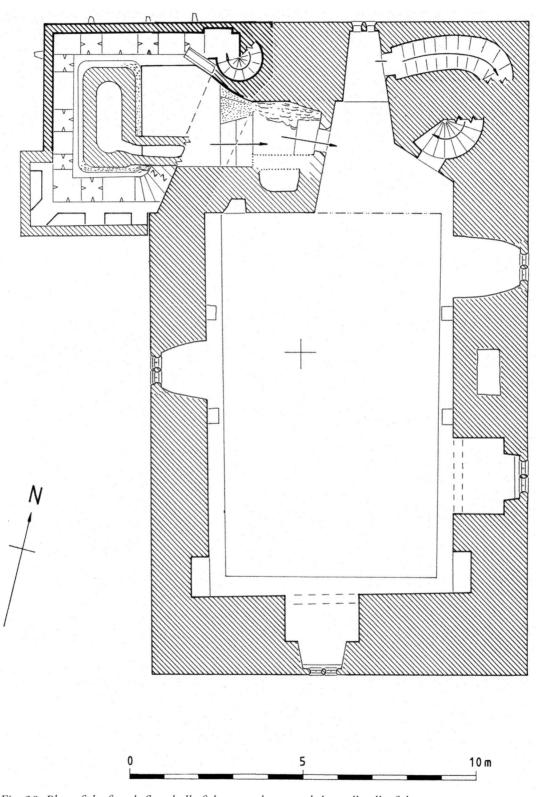

N

Fig. 30 Plan of the fourth-floor hall of the tower house and the wallwalk of the tower.

Fig. 31 The corbels supporting the west tower-house machicolation.

later fabric. This housing probably formed a small turret or lookout point on the north-west tower before the tower house was built. The diagonal wallwalk originally had a crow-stepped parapet, through which the modern stair joining both levels was driven (Fig. 32). The top of this earlier and partially demolished turret seems to have been left in a rough state and projects from under the later tower-house wall.

The tower-house battlement

The continuous wallwalk allowed a complete circuit. The large wire fence bedded in modern stonework should be mentally subtracted during the visit. The modern visitor is directed southwards from the head of the stair from the north-west tower towards the south walk and the Blarney Stone.

The wallwalk is six-sided (Fig. 33). The builders chose to balance the diagonal bridge with a similar arrangement on the north-east angle (Fig. 33) and the eastern chamfer oversails a quite different wall plan below. The builders realised halfway up that the turret they envisaged would obstruct the wallwalk, and a reduced turret was therefore built.

The wallwalk seems still to be substantially as executed in Period 2, although some reordering may have been carried out (see below). The 'valley system' is in principle like that used on the north-west tower but more sophisticated. The vast raised paving slabs (saddlestones) must weigh

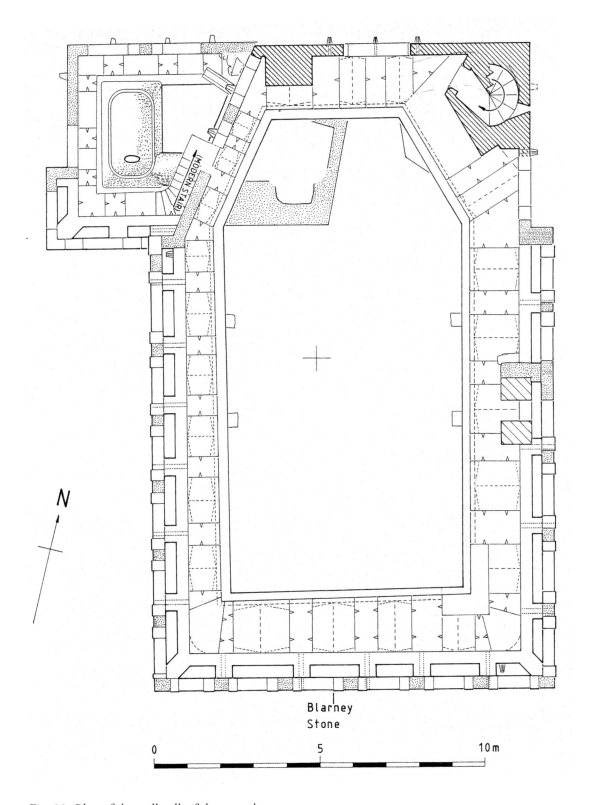

N

Blarney
Stone

0   5   10 m

Fig. 32 Plan of the wallwalk of the tower house.

in the region of a tonne. Their treatment, if not their size, is constant. The raised slabs were originally pitched but are now rather worn. The pitched shape meant that rainwater ran onto the intermediate valley stones rather than onto the base of the parapet and wooden roof. Both types of slab employ raised lips to direct rainwater away from vulnerable areas. The timber wall plate of the roof butted against the inner margin of the slabs (the rebate is now filled with cement), but the lips protected the timber from damp penetration.

A variation in the gaps between machicolation corbels (Period 4) was due to variation in the size of the earlier saddlestones, which range from 1.16 to 1.32 metres in width (3 feet, 9 inches–4 feet, 4 inches) on the west wallwalk. The width of the valleys between the saddle stones varies from 0.69 to 0.91 metres (2 feet, 4inches–3 feet). The east wallwalk has raised slabs up to 1.43 metres in maximum width (4 feet 8 inches).

Fig. 33 The north end of the fourth-floor chamber from the battlements, showing the change of design above the door.

The earlier wallwalk was provided with projecting conical spouts of dressed stone (Period 2), and examples survive between the later corbels. The unaltered north walk retains three spouts and further examples project from the diagonal 'bridge' parapet (Fig. 32).

One can only speculate how these enormous blocks were lifted into position. A rotating crane with a boom would certainly have been required. Slings of stout ropes or scissors (great pincers of iron) may have provided the necessary grip. A capstan powered by animals may have provided the power required to hoist the great slabs up to the wallwalk through a system of pulleys. It is easy to imagine the difficulties the crane operator and builders must have had positioning the corbel components into the southern angles. Slots were quarried deep into the angles to firmly hold the corbels in place; the relatively thin north wall of the tower house must have been judged too frail for such radical treatment.

The frequently pictured machicolations were probably built by the sixteenth Lord, Cormac Mc Dermot Mor Mac Carthy, in a period when the gun had already superseded traditional siege warfare; they were therefore primarily ornamental status symbols. Their real function was to eject rainwater away from the wall face below. The parapet rests on mighty corbels (Fig. 31), each assembled from three to five blocks of Cork limestone. Lintels with an average length of 2.3 metres (7 feet 6 inches) span between the corbels but do not quite meet; the slight gaps formed rainwater outlets from the valleys. A 'stub' inner parapet (Fig. 34) forms a safety barrier and is perforated at regular intervals to let the rainwater through.

It is now possible to catch a first glimpse of the Blarney Stone on the south wallwalk. The stone is identical to the other lintels except for its iron reinforcement to counteract past damage. Although the machicolation on this side of the tower house is noticeably irregular from below (Fig. 15), there is no evidence to suggest the stone has ever been disturbed from its position.

The parapet is finely crenellated with dressed stone. Each crow-stepped merlon had a central wedge-shaped coping stone, but these have been pushed off over the years. The parapets were recently repointed by a steeplejack (Fitzgerald 1999, p. 15). Musket loops were rather sparingly supplied in the parapets near the south angles.

The turret on the north-east angle, being the highest point, formed a lookout post; this was the home of the previously honoured Blarney Stone. The spout on its east side dates it to the first phase of the tower house (Period 2). It is now shorn of its parapet but was intact until the mid–nineteenth century. Windele mentions six steps that allowed one to climb up and kiss the (then) Blarney Stone (1839, p. 235) that was embedded in the parapet (Ch. 9). The steps seem to have been stone 'rungs' rather than a stair proper; these were broken off, perhaps at the same time that the parapet was removed (Fig. 32).

Perhaps the most peculiar feature on the battlements is a structure like a small Roman triumphal arch which partially obstructs the east wallwalk and which must be later than it. This was identified by the *Archaeological Inventory* as a bellcote with a chimney flue (Power 1997, p. 359). It must form the outlet of

Fig. 34   The west wallwalk and battlements, showing machicolation openings.

fireplaces in the first- and third-floor chambers of the tower house. The fanciful structure we see today probably replaces an earlier chimney, of which the lower part may survive. A 1796 Aquatint of Blarney Castle by Alken (National Library of Ireland of Ireland, Irish Topographical prints and original drawings, 171 TB) appears to show miniature crenellations on this structure.

Fig. 34 The surviving north end of the fourth-floor barrel vault, showing the embedded angle of the north-west tower below.

Masonry provision for the roof

A roof may have survived until about 1800, appearing as a point behind the parapet in a 1794 view of the tower (Fig. 10). Although a decorative crow-stepped 'false gable' was recorded in 1797 by Holmes (Fig. 8), this had no connection with the roof. The seating of the roof shows it was of hipped construction. The south end of the roof formed a single hip but the north end was polygonal in plan. Three sloping triangular faces rested against the main roof at points corresponding to the intersections of the chamfers.

What can be said of the timber roof structure? A continuous wall plate lay in the rebate (now filled in) against the ends of the wallwalk slabs. Other than this, reconstruction is speculative. The roof was probably built without wall risers or other types of bracing below the level of the eaves. It may be that massive tie beams spanned the fourth-floor hall chamber at regular intervals. Each tie beam may have supported a central crown strut, which in turn supported horizontal collars (Fig. 18). These provided bracing for the principal rafters; the full number of trusses is unknown but it may have been four. At least two were provided with additional support from braces supported on crude inserted corbels: probably a repair. A central louvre allowed smoke to escape from the hearth of the chamber below.

The roof was probably slated in its later days as we know was the case elsewhere in Ireland. The contract for a tower house built for the Ormonds, the Muskerry's peers, survives from 5 April 1547 and mentions that 'the roof be substantially covered with slate' (Ormond deeds; cited McKenna 1984, p. 12). Slates have also been found in several recent excavations of tower houses such as Barryscourt Castle (Monk and Tobin 1991, p. 43).

A curving stair in the west side of the north-east turret leads down to the fourth floor.

The tower-house fourth-floor hall

The stairs open onto a small irregular annex; a railing protects visitors from the sharp drop down through two floorless chambers below. At the bottom the second (stone-vaulted) floor can be seen. A marked step or offset marks the fourth floor. The east walls of this chamber and the one below it diverge by about 30 centimetres (1 foot) over their length; another of the 'adjustments' visible throughout the tower house (Ch. 11).

This floorless chamber, wider and longer than all others in the castle, strikes even the uninitiated as something special. It was entered from the north. The traditional image of the hall as seen in baronial castles springs to mind, but the features of the chamber tell a different story. It was obvious from the outside that, with one exception, the window mouldings are later than the embrasures that contain them. Traces of the old openings can still be identified. The external examination showed how the single-light sill of the Period 2 south window survives below the later one (p. 90–1).

The chamber survives much as it was built. From the battlements, the chamber can be seen to follow the polygonal lines of the wallwalk. It was recognised long ago that this chamber once had a stone-vaulted floor (Coleman 1895, p. 23), part of which survives at the north end (Fig. 35). The removal of this vault is best described in the context of the chamber below.

The hall once extended further to the north, but a partition wall incorporating a chimney flue (destroyed) was inserted in Period 4, shortening the hall. This created a passage to the kitchen. The other side of the heavily-restored door in the partition wall is

Fig. 36 The north-west corner of the fourth-floor chamber from the battlements.

Fig. 37 The south-east corner of the fourth-floor chamber from the battlements, showing the corner press.

visible from the kitchen (Fig. 31). The passage owes its present appearance (Fig. 36) to the removal or fall of an inserted chimney stack (Period 4) that once stood next to this passage. Subsequent 'tidying up' reveals that the rough mortar render of the fourth-floor chamber was applied *before* the building of the kitchen passage.

The spiral stair of the tower house, glimpsed from the entrance lobby and one of the castle's most impressive features, stops abruptly at the door into the hall making it impossible for enemies to bypass it. This interruption is also seen at Kilcrea Castle (Fig. 41b).

The function of the fourth floor

Modern writers usually call the top floor of tower houses the 'hall'. The Irish used the loanword '*halla*' in the fifteenth century (Simms 1999, p. 8) but we have no idea if this term was used for this type of chamber. The identification of this chamber as a chapel (Hillyard 1959, p. 6) can be discounted. It presumably derives from the pious assumption that the arched corner recesses or presses are liturgical in function. Both have been enlarged with arches of mortar.

Crawford Woods correctly identified this as the banqueting hall (1896, p. 343). A shelf in the south-east corner held the drinking vessels, while the south-west press held a safe for the fabled Muskerry plate. The chieftain's table ran along the south wall so he and his entourage could face out into the chamber. Here the Muskerry bards and other *ollúna* could enjoy the right generally enjoyed by their kind of sitting at the shoulder of the chieftain and sharing his plate and cup (Simms 1978, p. 89). Several poems survive in which bards apologise to the chieftain for their behaviour the night before.

A hearth in the centre of the hall allowed simple roasts and boiling cauldrons to be tended at the heart of the feast. Unusually, no wall fireplace was ever added to this chamber (in contrast to Kilcrea Castle) and the hearth seems to have been retained until the vaulted floor was removed at an unknown date.

As Gaelic society changed in the late sixteenth century, with the introduction of full-time servants and professional garrisons into the household, halls were updated to reflect this and the creation of at least two segregated dining areas is a feature of the late tower houses (Samuel 1998, p. 120–22). To bring Blarney Castle into line with these changes required serious structural interventions. The flue of a new fireplace was forced up through the fourth-floor vault. The flue had to be built *within* the old hall and the opportunity was taken to enclose the area north of this obstruction; this formed a passage to the new kitchen in the north-west tower (Period 4). A shelf, perhaps for plate or spirits or dry goods, was cut into the north wall of the passage (Fig. 33) which was probably used as a servery area.

The main spiral stair

It is now possible to walk down the main stair in the castle (Fig. 39). This stair of over ninety steps is of a more comfortable width than the Black Stairs but is still quite tricky to descend. Each tread of highly polished Cork limestone is 19.6 centimetres (7.75 inches) high, much higher than

the modern norm. A visitor should clutch the rope firmly. Each tread is a single triangular block, neatly chamfered below; the treads fit together to form a smooth ceiling. Eighteen treads form a full turn (helix) with a width of 2.35 metres (7 feet 8 inches) near the base. Higher up, the rate of ascent becomes sharper, with twenty treads per turn.

The stair is lit by square-headed loops deeply set in splays. The openings appear on alternate sides of the north-east angle. These lacked glass, like all the windows of the tower house (Period 2).

Fig. 38 The main spiral stair from below, showing the manner of assembly.

Third-floor garderobe chamber

The problem of human waste was dealt with by simple chutes in the north wall (see above) but ventilation was necessary, making use of the prevailing south-west winds, to control the stench. Although there are two well-ventilated garderobes, there is no evidence of any social or sexual segregation in the modern sense. A direct view into either chamber from the stairs was, however, avoided.

The visitor enters the upper garderobe at the level of the third floor. A common passage leads to the main chamber and, at the right hand, onto stairs that climb in darkness around the curve of the spiral stair and into the vaulted chamber. The lavatory seat and its sides of timber have vanished, but the supporting offset indicates a seat running along the outer wall over a vertical shaft that comprised the sewage system. The shaft descends several metres before opening onto the exterior. The projecting slab cast the waste away from the castle wall face and into the quarry. Three users may have sat on holes in the seat at the same time. Small openings, one a rough slit and the other a square-headed chamfered loop, light the chamber. The east side of the tower (Period 1) forms the west wall. Because the earlier tower incorporates a shallow projecting turret for the Black Stairs, the chamber has in consequence a highly irregular plan.

High over the chamber door the mouth of a channel can be seen that runs several metres south-west to a small rough opening in the south wall. This vent allowed a through-flow of fresh air into the chamber.

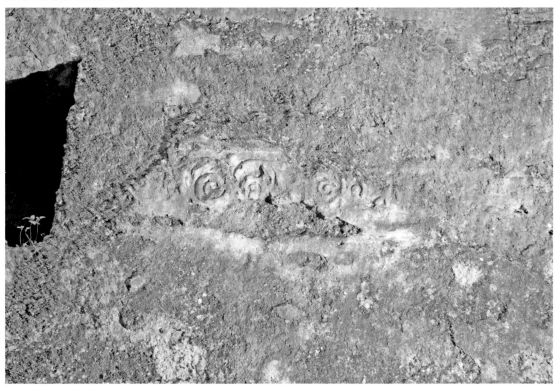

Fig. 39 Remnants of the plaster ornament in the second-floor chamber.

Tower-house third-floor chamber

Returning to the passage, the visitor bears right to the barred entrance to the now floorless main third-floor chamber. Behind them a dressed rectangular loop overlooks the valley east of the castle.

Looking into the chamber one can see where the floor rafters rested on wall plates, which were supported by rows of well-cut corbels. These and the offsets or ledges below them were provided from the outset (Period 2). The difference in level between the two represents the thickness of the vanished timber wall plates. Rafters resting on these, not the offsets, brought the floor up to the level of the door embrasures (Fig. 18). Above these offsets the walls of the chamber are irregular, except for a strip immediately above them, which includes dressed quoins at the bases of the embrasures. It follows that the barrel vault's stump, which can be seen to the right, once sprang from these wall faces. The stump now appears as a deceptively neat arch over the north end of the chamber. The print of woven hurdle centring and the torn edge of the vault are visible. This barrel vault once extended across the chamber but is now cut flush with the southeast angle of the early tower (Period 1), clearly visible from below (Fig. 35). A plaster finish has survived on the north wall and the underside of the vault 'stump'. It covered the hurdle centring, which was trapped, ultimately decaying in position. The plaster is not original (see below).

The chamber's original north wall is masked by an inserted wall containing a chimney flue which served a magnificent fireplace in the chamber below (Period 4). It was necessary to shorten the chamber to accommodate it. The inserted wall incorporates a ledge that formed the basis of a vanished timber bench. The rough string course of slabs below was probably built under the earlier floor joist, and gave it additional support.

These alterations can be dated to Period 4. The plaster must be contemporary or later. The chamfered jambs of what appear to be a blocked fireplace survive in the east wall. A timber lintel observed over it (Power 1997, pp. 358–60) may be a repair carried out after the removal of the vault. It follows that the loss of the vault occurred before the tower house fell out of use. This raises the possibility that the removal was intentional. Smoke from the fireplace (Period 2) issued from the peculiar bellcote on the battlements. This fireplace is apparently the only one built as part of the tower house. The vault was replaced by a timber floor (Period 6) that rested on a convenient offset (Period 2).

It would have been necessary to run subsidiary (dormer) vaults at right angles from the vault to accommodate the windows and doors, because the barrel vault once occupied the full height of the chamber. The embrasures were cut back into their present form after the fall or removal of the vault. A fragment of one of these subsidiary arches can be seen over the door into the chamber.

The improvements carried out between approximately 1584 and 1616 show the work of at least two masons. The three windows are all enlarged but retain earlier embrasures. The sides seem to have been scaffolded separately by a mason who then replaced the windows in a distinctive manner. A separate hand can be detected in the windows of the south and east walls.

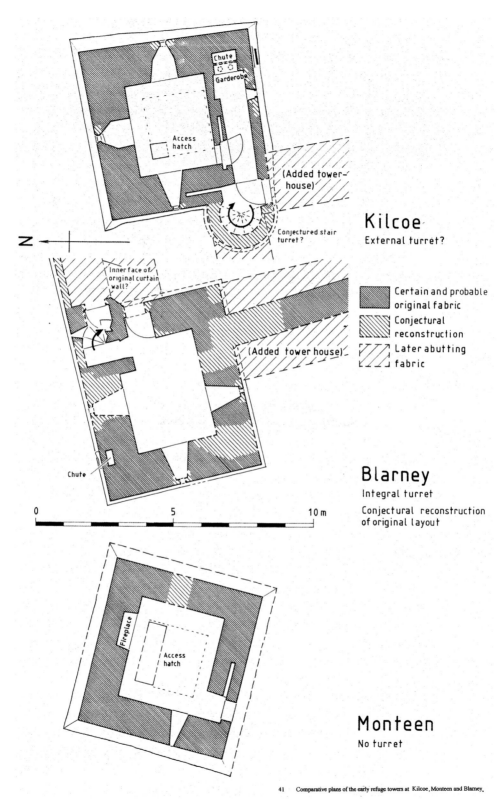

Fig. 40 *Comparative plans of the early refuge towers at (a) Kilcoe, (b) Blarney and (c), Monteen.*

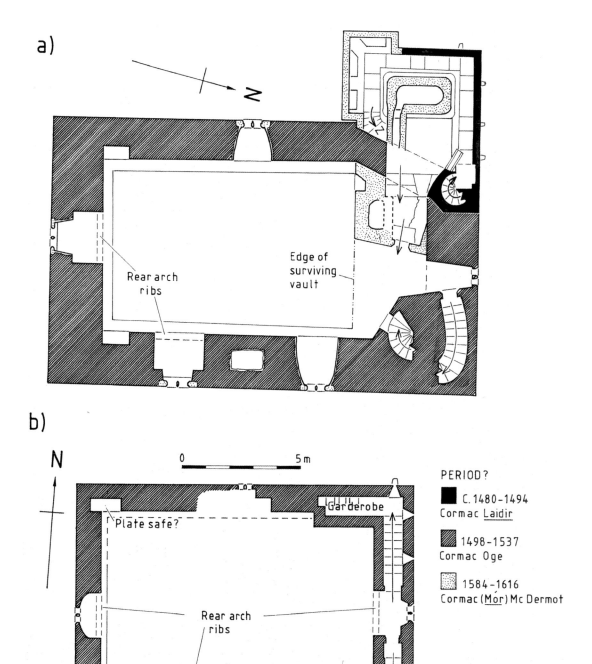

Fig. 41 Comparative plans of the fourth-floor halls at Blarney (a) and Kilcrea (b).

Second floor

The chamber floor rests on the great barrel vault, and although any floor surfaces are masked by a functional coat of asphalt it is possible to examine the chamber in more detail than usual. It is reached from the next door off the spiral stair through a passage in the east wall. Traces can be seen of a hinged security grille, which would impede any attackers who had forced an entrance to the stairs. The constricted end of the passage curves around into the chamber, but the altered entranceway has been repaired in brick. A solitary rectangular opening, partially blocked, lights the passage.

In its original state the passage was short, and one entered the chamber through a fine stone doorway near the stair, part of which survives, though blocked (Fig. 27). The passage was later quarried southwards to create the present curved entranceway.

Slight traces of rich stucco ornamentation survive towards the south-eastern angle (Fig. 39). A frieze or cornice of acanthus-derived ornament ran below the ceiling joists, probably below a plaster ceiling concealing the Period 2 joists. This plasterwork is probably seventeenth century (Period 5). It may be conjectured that this chamber became a 'high status' hall or dining chamber, partly usurping the main fourth-floor hall in Period 4. Main occupancy gradually shifted down floor by floor, reflecting a greater desire for comfort and convenience, from the later sixteenth century.

A single gigantic fireplace, the chief alteration made to this chamber during its history, was built against the north wall. To do this, an entire new north wall had to be built 'inboard' of its predecessor. Enough survives of the fireplace to show that it employed a joggled flat-arch lintel assembled from a series of stepped blocks. A shallow mantelshelf of stone ran above this. The fireplace seems to have survived intact into the early nineteenth century. Windele wrote that 'its chimney is elaborately worked, and the fireplace where the flames of many an oak arose; "and the tales of heroes were told," is about 12" wide' (1839, p. 235). Sadly, the joggled lintel must have subsequently collapsed. A hidden relieving arch of stone reduced the strain on the lintel. The same technique was used in the contemporary kitchen (see above). Although this chamber was not a kitchen, the fireplace could have been used for roasting meat – it was certainly large enough to spit-roast a side of beef.

A much humbler and narrower fireplace was constructed in the wreck of the old fireplace, and most of the flue and opening was built up after the castle had ceased to be inhabited. As in the decorative garden buildings in great houses, which also contain fireplaces, this suggests that the ruins might have been used for Victorian picnics.

A small press of uncertain date at the south-east corner is covered by a segmental arch. In Period 4 the east window and its embrasure were built from scratch and at the same time the southern window embrasure was quarried outwards on the west side to allow the construction of a three-light opening. The original two-light sill (Period 2) is still visible outside below the present window. A very tall ogival loop (Period 2) survives in the west wall next to the door leading down to the passage in the haunch of the vault. (This passage, described earlier, leads to the Earl's Chamber in the north-west tower.) The very low and hollow sill of the loop was probably intended to serve as a channel to allow dirty water escape from the floor; it still allows rainwater to run off. The loop and the chamfered doorway with its fine pointed arch and stops are characteristic of the early sixteenth century (Period 2).

Though the two-light window to the north of the ogival loop has been massively enlarged, the south embrasure splay is original. The peculiar disc with a small slot carved on the mullion may have held a pivoted shutter-fastening catch.

The evolution of this chamber from a poorly lit and unheated space to a convivial chamber with a great fireplace, large glazed windows and fashionable stucco ornament illustrates how the developing stratification of Irish society was directly reflected in the architecture (Ch. 3).

This is the last substantial chamber in the castle tour. Only now is it possible to see the traditional route to the north-west tower from the main entrance.

Third-floor annex chamber

Several steps down, the visitor enters a small barrel-vaulted chamber in the thickness of the north wall. The walls are covered with a well-preserved render. A tall rectilinear loop with a slop stone below it pierces the north wall and, as in the chamber above, the stair turret of the Period 1 tower forms the west wall. A small hole runs between the two at a sharp angle (Fig. 27) so as to provide no view. Crawford Woods suggested that this chamber was either a dungeon or a sickroom, perhaps both, and ingeniously added that an invalid lying in the chamber would be able to hear mass in the nearby chapel in the north-west tower (1896, p. 341) through this 'speaking tube'. Guides once identified this as the Baroness's Chamber (Hillyard 1959, p. 6) perhaps to introduce balance, there already being an Earl's Chamber. The identification seems fanciful, given the absence of evidence for a timber door, but such identifications can rarely be rejected out of hand, although strictly it would be the Countess's Chamber. All we can truly say is that the presence of such a chamber was dictated by structural requirements – some use was then found for it.

Garderobe chamber intermediate between first and second floors

This barrel-vaulted garderobe chamber resembles the one above it. Such is the height occupied by the great second-floor vault that the builders were able to fit this chamber in the north wall, and it therefore does not correspond to any of the main floor levels.

It might be asked why the approach to this chamber from the spiral stair is so torturous (Fig. 25) for it is necessary to leave the spiral stair through an entrance in its south side. The passage then describes a hairpin before returning northwards to the chamber. The reason is that it was not possible to open a door directly off the spiral stair at a suitable level, except by these means. As in the garderobe above, a direct view into the chamber was thus avoided.

Etiquette seems to have dictated that it was fine to be seen in the garderobe by one's fellow user(s), but not by passers-by.

The chamber, like the other one, has a vent running through the whole thickness of the east wall of the tower house to encourage the entry of the south-west wind to provide very desirable ventilation. The walls are thickly rendered, preserving the outline of the vanished timber seat on a ledge. The seat originally extended further to the west, but the redundant part of the ledge was subsequently rendered over. Moss (the medieval equivalent of quilted paper) may have been stored in the recess in the wall opposite. The lower part of the loop over the seat was enlarged late in the history of the castle (Period 6) to take a glass window, the hole being finished in brick. The tall rectilinear loop has a slop stone and may have served as a urinal.

The murder hole

Continuing the descent, the visitor sees a small door through the south side of the stairwell. A short flight of stairs leads down to the site of the original east entrance to the first floor (Fig. 23). The present doorway is apparently enlarged. The flight is partially blocked at the base, perhaps to prevent those walking down the stairs in the dark from falling into the murder hole, now blocked. This feature allowed the castle's defenders to assail from above any attackers who had broken through the main entrance below. The passage may have continued further south to another chamber entrance. The two-light window is in the Elizabethan style but is probably eighteenth- or nineteenth-century reconstruction work.

The passage between the spiral stairs

It is now possible to walk down the spiral stair to a passage leading to the Black Stairs. This runs the length of the north wall and it is probable that the earlier curtain wall was re-employed as its north side. The doorway leading to the Black Stairs has the finely dressed details characteristic of Period 2. The integration of the two towers presented some problems to the builders. The plan (Fig. 23) conjectures which parts derive from the Period 1 fabric.

The entrance to the original refuge tower (Period 1) was in the east side to the south of the projecting stair turret (Crawford Woods 1896, p. 340). This entrance was, as is usual in these structures, raised high above the ground for security (p. 96). The builders of the tower house apparently aimed to make their new passage run to this door from the spiral stair. However, the original entrance was bypassed and instead another door was built into the north side of the passage. The new door required a stair to be quarried northwards through the curtain wall (Period 1) so as to curve around to meet the Black Stairs (Fig. 23). It is likely that it led to where a door originally opened out onto the wallwalk of the curtain wall.

It has long been established that the north curtain wall of the courtyard castle survives more or less to its full height, i.e. to the first floor, embedded in the tower house (Crawford Woods

1896, p. 240). We know this because the north-east corner of the north-west tower was only free-standing from first-floor level, as indicated by its quoins. The outer wall face is greatly altered at this point, but one of the loops of the turret survives next to a much larger modern opening (p. 105).

Retracing their steps, the visitor is now able to leave the castle through the bottom of the spiral stair. The foot of the stairs originally had two doorways, one leading in to the ground-floor chamber and the other leading into the entrance lobby (p. 99). This gave defenders a means of escape, should they be caught on the ground floor (Fig. 20), but it was perhaps seen as a potential weakness and was blocked off

CHAPTER 11

A Summary of Blarney Castle's Context and Development

A VISUAL SUMMARY of the building sequence can be seen in Fig. 18, which indicates the amount of alteration that has occurred since the castle was built.

The courtyard castle (Period 1), 1480–94

A courtyard castle was built either soon after Blarney came into the hands of the Muskerry family in about 1480 (Sweetman 1999), or, less probably, by the Lombards shortly before. The timber lacing in the structure (Fig. 25) could be dated by scientific means. Either way, it did not exist in its original form for long. Similarities between the Mac Carthy castles at Kilcrea and Blarney are apparent in details such as the corbelling used at Kilcrea Castle to widen the wallwalk (Samuel 1998, p. 629), which is closely matched in the Period 1 tower at Blarney. Since Kilcrea was built in about 1500 this indicates fairly rapid transition from the Period 1 courtyard castle to the Period 2 tower house.

For brevity, we will call the corner tower just 'the tower' to distinguish it from the tower house. The north-west tower, the west part of the north curtain wall and the base of a south-west tower survive of the original courtyard castle. The tower house was subsequently built into the west side of this castle. It is probable that a west curtain wall is entombed within the west wall of the tower house (Fig. 19). Quarrying has removed all the terrain on which the east part of the original stronghold stood, but an educated guess is that it was quadrangular in plan, with towers at each angle. As well as the surviving tower at the north-west angle, a stump of a south-western tower projects from the south wall of the tower house (Fig. 16). The surviving tower may have been larger than the others. It was flush with the north curtain wall but projected westwards to allow flanking fire along the west curtain wall. The other towers may have been similarly arranged. It has been suggested that the tower was the first stage in the construction of a tower house (Sweetman 1999, p. 161) but this cannot be. The tower's eastward-facing openings, noted as long ago as 1896, disprove this. They are consistent with an open courtyard, surrounded by a battlement reached from the Black Stairs (Ch. 10). Perhaps a free-standing timber hall stood in the courtyard.

The building techniques used are broadly those used in sixteenth-century tower houses (the cornice that runs around the highest chamber of Kilcrea Castle being a case in point).

The decision to retain the tower suggests it was more important than its lost counterparts. The difficulties of unravelling the origin of the tower-house form in Ireland have been described by T.E. McNeill (1997, pp. 202–5) but it is worth comparing this Period 1 tower with other 'refuge towers'. This was a type of structure peculiar to Co. Cork and, to judge from its relationship to other subsequent buildings, was a predecessor of the full-blown tower house in this county (Samuel 1998, p. 732). These buildings were intended only for brief occupation when any threat arose. They lacked defensive features and were meant simply to provide protection until a threat subsided. In some cases they were 'enlarged' to form part of a later, more substantial tower house; Blarney is by no means unique, in this.

'Refuge towers' are distinguished from 'true' tower houses by their relatively small size: seldom more than 6 or 7 metres square, and their square or nearly square plan. They were probably only used in emergencies. They consist of no more than several small square chambers, one above the other; a sharp batter was required for stability. There are few uniform features: the Blarney tower, for example, rejoiced in the luxury of a stair and a garderobe (Fig. 40b) while Monteen, a refuge tower, lacked both but had fireplaces (Fig. 40c). They usually had a raised entrance in one wall but even this is not universal: the Mac Carthy Muskerry stronghold of Castlemore (Gillman 1892c, p. 217) had a ground-floor entrance and (apparently) two such towers. The first floor was usually formed by a vault, with a hatch giving access to a square shaft within the hollow base. This perhaps served as a cistern or grain store. The excavated shaft at Kilcoe Castle, near Schull, a Clan Dermot Mac Carthy tower house, expanded from a refuge tower, is dry with a flat floor cut in the rock (Jeremy Irons, pers. comm.). A prevalent feature was the barrel-vaulting of alternate floors to create fire barriers. At Monteen access was only gained to the upper floors by ladders passing through hatches in the vaults, while at Kilcoe a spiral stair probably provided access to the lower floors, while intramural stairs were used further up (Fig. 40a).

Kilcoe Castle shows a similar pattern of alteration to Blarney but Monteen remained free-standing throughout its history. The base of the Blarney tower is probably also hollow and a filled-in hatch may one day be revealed in the stone floor of the Earl's Chamber.

Refuge towers were soon superseded by larger tower houses. It seems that rapid societal change led to the widespread adoption of tower houses, whose design permitted permanent occupation. The courtyard castle at Blarney, barely completed, was soon obsolete and much of its material must have gone into the tower house that supplanted it.

The tower house (Period 2), 1498–1537

The building of Kilcrea Castle and Blarney is traditionally attributed to Cormac Laidir but the gunloops in both structures suggest a later date and his son, Cormac Oge, is more likely to be responsible (Ch. 4). The common history of the buildings is reflected in their architecture.

Kilcrea, unlike Blarney, was built on a 'greenfield' site and was barely altered subsequently. A single guiding hand is indicated by its carefully proportioned design regulated by the Statute Foot (Samuel 1998, p. 625). The pervasive corrections and irregularities seen at Blarney are absent. At Kilcrea the tenacious Cork limestone is carefully shaped into neat blocks set in excellent mortar. This barely ruined building therefore has the air of a concrete bunker; it lacks the soft crumbling mossiness seen in most Irish ruins. In contrast, Blarney's walls are built from undressed rubble, randomly coursed and supported only by the strength of the mortar. Dressings are limited to angles and openings.

Kilcrea has similarities with many of the magnificent early-sixteenth-century tower houses built by the Earls of Desmond and their subordinate clans in East Cork, Limerick and Tipperary. Its ground plan closely resembles those of Conna, East Cork, and Garraunboy, Co. Limerick (ibid., p. 198). In West Cork lack of resources and the fragmentation of lordships discouraged the building of such 'super tower houses' (ibid). Kilcrea is sited in an attractive valley with no strategic strength but capable of supporting huge herds and other agricultural activities. Like those of the great majority of tower houses (McNeill 1997, p. 220), its site was simply convenient for normal life.

The presence of vaults at second- and fourth-floor level is a 'luxury' feature rarely seen in the tower houses of Cork. It has been noticed by McNeill that a substantial minority of tower houses in Limerick and Tipperary have a vault over more than one floor and he raises the possibility that this is connected with date as well as regional influence (ibid., p. 213). It has become evident that the final West Cork tower houses usually lack any vaults (Samuel 1998, p. 117). A date before the third quarter of the sixteenth century is probable.

At Blarney the incorporation of an earlier tower and curtain walls led to several peculiarities, including the north–south orientation. In Co. Cork tower houses are usually oriented approximately east–west on the strike of the rock (ibid., p. 98). The short-axis dimension of the plan at both tower houses is nearly identical, being about 11.95 metres (39 feet 2 inches) at Kilcrea (Samuel 1998, 633) and 11.99 metres (39 feet 4 inches) at Blarney (Leask 1951, Fig. 78). Blarney, however, lacks a defined base batter.

In the earlier Cork tower houses the fourth-floor hall was of paramount importance and had a standard layout. Blarney and Kilcrea can be compared more easily by turning them so that they have the same orientation (Fig. 41), with the main spiral stair at the 'bottom right'.

The first revelation is that the Kilcrea hall is *larger* than that of Blarney; indicating the importance this now little-regarded building once had in the pecking order of Muskerry strongholds. Its layout probably reflects the etiquette and customs of lost timber halls. Although it has been asserted otherwise (Sweetman 1999, p. 161), the windows we see today in this floor at Blarney have all been altered except on the north side. Only the right-hand window in the 'bottom' wall at Blarney is a completely late-sixteenth-century creation (Period 4). At Kilcrea the 'bottom' (south) window was exceptionally large and may have had tracery within its arched head.

Paired ogival lights sheltered by square hood moulds are otherwise used. All except the north had the unusual ribbed rear arches (Samuel 1998, p. 629) also seen at Blarney.

Although the two halls are not identical, the two recesses at the 'left-hand' corners indicate similarity of use. 'Shelves' and 'presses' usually occur at this point in the plan (ibid., p. 85). The two presses at Kilcrea occupy the same point in the plan as at Blarney, but take the form of a long, low 'shelf' at the south angle and a large oblong 'press' penetrating beyond the corner opposite (Fig. 41b). The Blarney presses were later enlarged and given pointed arches of mortar to make them symmetrical.

Other points of similarity can be seen in the stairs and their relation to the fourth floor (Fig. 41). The creation of the spiral from single highly dressed blocks of Cork limestone is a rare extravagance. A shared peculiarity is the absence of a central 'mast' of the sort seen in English castles. Kilcrea retains a neat garderobe chamber with a triple seat in the north-east angle, but the retention of the earlier tower ruled out this arrangement at Blarney (Fig. 40a) and these chambers had to be provided at a lower level.

The battlements of Kilcrea, though greatly damaged, retain some of the shovel-shaped gutter blocks, pitched saddlestones and projecting rainwater outlets also used at Blarney (the latter rendered useless by the Period 4 machicolations). These freestone features are far more refined in their details than is usual in Cork tower houses. Both castles had hipped roofs without gables. Although it has been suggested that timber hoardings were not used in the later medieval period in Ireland (McNeill 1997, p. 218), evidence for them has been seen in Cork at, for example, Kilgobbin Castle (Samuel 1998, p. 86). Perhaps Kilcrea Castle and Blarney had such overhanging timber galleries on their battlements when first built, but in both cases the original parapet is gone.

The documented connection between the two strongholds (Nicholls 1993b, p. 173) is further supported by the shared masonry techniques and layout (including the basal dimension). Kilcrea is conceivably slightly earlier, although Blarney is certainly no slavish imitation. The builder of Blarney incorporated the existing building work where possible because the earlier stronghold was still fairly new. This allowed a series of private rooms, in contrast to Kilcrea where the 'stack' of huge chambers made privacy impossible.

Alterations to the tower house (Periods 3–5)

Period 3, 1525–50

The earliest alteration to the tower house was the addition of a fine oriel window in what can with good cause be identified as the Earl's Chamber.

Such oriels are very rare in Irish castles; the only known parallel is at Granagh Castle (Co. Kilkenny), a fine oriel dated between 1515 and 1539 (Grose 1991, p. 158). The Blarney example probably dates from the contemporary chieftainship (1537–65) of Teige Mac Cormac Oge Mac

Carthy. His often-widowed daughter Julia married, as her third husband, Edmund Butler, who was Lord Dunboyne, brother of the Earl of Ormond and lord of Granagh Castle (Fig. 4). (The Butler family (Ormond) were one of the few families important enough for the Mac Carthy Muskerrys to marry.) This link may have brought the oriel at Granagh to the attention of Teige Mac Cormac, which highlights how the study of Irish castles must be carried out with a full understanding of history, where this survives.

Period 4, 1584–1616

A great programme of window replacement, machicolation construction and fireplace insertion was carried out between 1584 and 1616 during the chieftainship of Cormac Mac Dermot Mor, the sixteenth lord. The glazed windows, with their square hood moulds, are clearly the result of English influence. The blurring of distinctions between the Irish ruling class, the 'Old English' and the 'New English' planters before the Nine Years War created a class of masons who were 'bilingual', providing both tower houses and defended manor houses as required by their different clients.

Period 5, 1616–41

By 1620 Cormac Oge Mac Carthy (seventeenth Lord) regarded Macroom Castle as his prime residence, but efforts were subsequently made to upgrade the old tower house at Blarney.

The late-sixteenth-century fireplace and the *c.* 1630s fireplace show how the Lord of Muskerry shifted the main focus of occupation progressively downwards, first to the second floor and finally to the first floor. The tower house seems to have been little used by the ruling family after about 1650; a 'new house of stone' was referred to in a 1654 Cromwellian survey (MacCarthy 1990, p. 162). This was in all probability the earliest part of the mansion, whose ruined shell survived more or less complete until about 1975.

Virtually no alterations to the tower house, except perhaps the addition of the bellcote, seem to have been carried out between the outbreak of Civil War in 1641 and the final confiscation of the Clancarty earldom over fifty years later. Some reinforcement of the bawn walls to make them more resistant to cannon fire is the only change that can be attributed to this period.

Continued occupation and the 'curation' of a ruin (Period 6), post 1703

The recent survey has revealed the amount of work that has been carried out over the centuries to preserve the structure; more importantly it has emphasised that the tower house was occupied, floored and roofed, into the modern period. Exterior slate-hanging, the insertion of casement windows and the reduction of great fireplaces to more practical dimensions indicate how the lower floors of the tower house were made habitable. These changes may have been carried out by one

Mr Beer who was living in the tower house in 1750 (Gillman 1892a, p. 37). He may have been a tenant of the Jefferyes, prior to the rebuilding of the seventeenth-century domestic wing in the 1760s (MacCarthy 1990, p. 162).

The removal of whatever remained of the roofs and floors seems to have been carried out in about 1800, and subsequent repairs were probably required as a result of damp penetration. Failure of the barrel vaults was countered by the wholesale removal of the upper vault. The (probably) connected collapse of the great central chimneystack and fireplace must have occurred soon after Windele's visit, and extensive repairs would have been required after this happened. The second-floor fireplace was rebuilt after this time. Two square-hooded windows on the east wall were probably built to replace openings which had been robbed of their stone. In the 1890s the fine Renaissance gate of the gatehouse was carefully reset, having been previously removed. The north-east turret was put 'out of bounds' in about 1870 and the steps removed. Reinforcement of the present Blarney Stone soon followed. Apart from the introduction of timber stairs, asphalt floors and railings, little has been done to the tower house since that time, apart from general attention to safety and the recent repointing of the parapet by a Limerick-based steeplejack (Fitzgerald 1999, p. 15).

Appendix: Castles mentioned in the text

Grid references to the locations of Co. Cork castles mentioned in the text where substantial remains survive are given below.

Note: The law on public right of way in Ireland is a contentious issue. There are very few rights of way in Ireland and anyone stepping onto land they do not own is technically a trespasser unless they can prove their entitlement to do so. The landowner is, however, liable for injuries suffered by the trespasser or recreational user. In the author's childhood walkers were tolerated, or at least ignored, but the law is now increasingly used as a tool to bar any walkers from private land, especially if it has a dangerous ruin on it!

Mention of a castle in this Appendix is therefore no guarantee of access, and permission to visit should be sought from the landowner, ideally in advance. All castles are explored at the able-bodied visitor's own risk. Bulls and inquisitive cattle are always a danger! Do not run from dogs. Wear suitable clothes and boots. Do not be discouraged but please do behave so as to ensure the next visitor is not turned away.

Ballea Castle (NGR W 7050 6300): Privately owned. This must be the oldest continuously inhabited house in Cork and still preserves its *yett* over the door.

Ballynacariga (NGR W 2875 5080): A National Monument.

Barryscourt (NGR W 8230 7240): A well-restored National Monument (check opening hours). Contact details: +353 (0)21 4882218 or +353 (0)21 4883864 (winter)

Carigadrochid (NGR W 4130 7230): Right next to the main road.

Carrigaphooka Castle (NGR W 2900 7300): A National Monument (open all hours).

Castlemore (NGR W 4440 6695): Very overgrown and picturesque, but rather hazardous.

Castle Salem (NGR W 2687 3860): Attached to a privately owned B&B but open to the public.

Kilcoe Castle (NGR W 0192 3282): Restored/inhabited and privately owned.

Kilcrea (NGR W 5050 6800): Situated on a dairy farm. (Kilcrea Abbey, a National Monument is nearby.)

Kilgobbin Castle (NGR W 5891 4999): Situated in an active farmyard. Interior inaccessible.

Monteen (NGR W 4307 4699): Situated on dairy farm.

Togher (NGR W 1963 5717): Situated on dairy farm. Interior inaccessible.

(This information was last verified in 1998.)

Glossary of Technical Terms

acanthus: a plant with a distinctive leaf used as decoration in classical architecture.

archlet: a little arch.

arriss: a sharp edge made by the meeting of two surfaces at different angles.

ashlar: worked stone, squared stone in regular courses.

astragal: an upright of either timber or iron in the centre of a window, to which glazing can be attached.

barrel vault: the simplest form of vault, consisting of a continuous vault of semi-circular or pointed section unbroken in its length by cross-vaults.

bartizan: an overhanging corner turret, supported on corbels.

base-batter: sloping wall surface, ascending from a wide base to a narrower superstructure. Found on the visible part of the building, not the foundation.

bastion: a projection at the angle of a fortification, from which the garrison can see and defend the ground before the walls or ramparts.

bellcote: a structure of timber or stone on the top of a building in which a bell is suspended.

bawn (from the Irish *bádhun*): a shelter for cattle; usually now used to denote the defensive buildings around a tower house, also used to protect livestock.

buttery: a chamber used for decanting and serving drinks.

Carmarthen arch: opening with a flat lintel. The lintel rests on two small corbels.

casement/casemented: a pivoted window inner frame attached to tile outer frame by hinges.

capstan: used for hoisting weights. A cylinder revolves on a vertical axis. Bars fixed or inserted into the cylinder are then pulled or pushed to wind a rope, from which the weight is suspended, around the cylinder.

centring (or centering): wooden framework used in arch or vault construction. It is removed or 'struck' when tile mortar has set.

chamfer: the removal of a right-angled corner to create a third face diagonal to the two other faces.

chamfer stop: an ornamental termination to a chamfer, bringing the edge back to a right angle.

collar: a horizontal beam connecting the opposing sides of a pitched roof.

coping: a trim on a wall or parapet designed to throw water off.

corbel: a projection from a wall that would have supported something, e.g., a floor.

coursed/courses: the laying of stone or bricks in horizontal bands.

courtyard castle: a 'soft-centred' castle, usually rectangular in plan and with no central keep.

crenellation: a battlemented parapet.

crown strut: a vertical timber bracing the upper and lower horizontal tie-beams in a truss.

crow-stepped: describes a parapet whose upper edge is cut into a series of steps.

curtain wall: the outer enclosing wall connecting the towers of a castle.

cyma recta: an 'S' section Renaissance moulding, often used to form an overhanging cornice.

date stone: an inscribed stone recording the date of building work.

dendrochronological dating: the thickness of wood laid down in a tree each year will be greatly affected by climatic variation. This allows the exact dating of timber by relating tree-rings from old wood to dated 'ring sequences'.

deadspot: a place outside the walls which cannot be seen by defenders.

dormer: a window built within a sloping roof.

drawbeam: a length or bolt of timber drawn along the inner face of a door to both lock and reinforce it. A hole will be provided for it in the side of the door.

dropped keystone: projects below the soffit of an arch as an ornamental device.

embrasure: a door or window recess.

enfilade: a fire from guns which sweeps an area from end to end. Guns are positioned to provide 'enfilading fire'.

forebuilding: an additional building against the tower containing the entrance staircase.

freestone: unbedded, easily worked stone.

garderobe: a lavatory.

glacis: a slope in the outer defence, made of earth or stone, eliminating the deadspots.

gunnery: all things pertaining to the subject of managing guns.

gunloop: a hole in the wall shaped to admit a gun barrel.

harling: an external waterproof coating; normally a form of plaster but can also be of mortar.

hipped roof: a roof with sloping rather than vertical ends.

hoarding: a defensive wooden gallery supported on brackets at the top of the tower.

hood mould: a moulding projecting over a window or doorway, either square or following the shape of the arch.

jamb: the side of a window or door.

joggled: stones joined up with a projection on one and a shelf in its neighbour.

keystone: the central stone at the highest point of an arch.

label stop: termination of a hood mould, normally to either side of the window head.

lacing: reinforcement of a stone or brick wall with horizontal timbers.

lintel: a horizontal beam above a door, window or fireplace.

loop: a small narrow window.

louvre: a shuttered opening in a roof to allow smoke to escape.

machicolation: an opening in the floor of the parapet through which missiles could be dropped, more permanent than a hoarding.

merlon: the solid, upstanding part of a crenellation.

mullion: a vertical bar dividing the lights of a window.

musketloop: a narrow slit opening to fire a musket through.

murder hole: a defensive feature consisting of an aperture over a door or entrance lobby through which intruders could be attacked from above.

newel: the central pillar of a spiral stair.

offset: a break or ledge on the face of the wall where the wall above is reduced in thickness (OED).

ogival: based on an ogee, i.e., a curve shaped like an elongated 's'.

outdoor relief: Labouring work, sometimes on public works, offered to the poor, to keep them out of the workhouse.

outside jaunting cars: horsedrawn carts arranged to seat two rows of passengers sitting back to back and facing outwards.

pintle: a pin or bolt on which something turns.

piscina: a shallow stone bowl set in the south wall of a church chancel and used to wash communion vessels.

pitcher: a chisel with a wide blunt blade.

press: a recess in a tower-house wall, usually cuboid.

punch: a pointed chisel.

purlin: a horizontal, longitudinal beam used in roofs, flooring, etc.

quoin: a stone cut to form the outer angles of a building.

rebate: a longitudinal rectangular recess or groove designed to receive a timber.

relieving arch: an arch placed in the wall over an opening to relieve it of the weight of the masonry above.

render: a coating of plaster or mortar.

reveal: a side of an opening or recess which is at right angles to the face (OED).

revetment: a wall of timber or stone used to support a terrace or rampart.

saddlestone: (in this context) a raised paving slab used to channel rainwater into gutters.

scantling: dimensions of a piece of timber in breadth and thickness; denotes a square piece of timber.

scissors: scissor-shaped grappling irons for lifting stones. Tension on the attached rope causes the irons to tighten.

skewback: the sloping surface on which either extremity of an arch rests (OED).

slighting: destroying or damaging a stronghold to make it useless.

slop stone: a hole in the wall through which unwanted liquids were poured, usually onto a projecting slab.

soakaway: a hole in the wall into which water could be poured to drain into the wall's thickness.

soffit: the under surface of a lintel, vault or arch (OED).

solar: private apartment of a castle or tower house's owner.

spandrel: a triangular space between the curve of an arch and its rectangular frames.

squint: (correctly) a small opening cut through a church wall to allow a view of the high altar, but also used of any small spyhole.

Statute Foot: a measure of 30.48 centimetres traditionally believed to be instituted by Henry I (1100–1135) and unchanged since. It may be an older Saxon unit formally adopted by the Normans in preference to their own units.

stooling: the flat surface of a sill on which a jamb or mullion rests.

stop: a method used in carpentry or masonry to end a chamfer; at Blarney it resembles a pyramid cut in half diagonally from the apex.

stub parapet: a low wall used at Blarney on the battlements to prevent people from falling down the machicolation openings

string course: a projecting horizontal course in a wall, often moulded.

tally stick: a method historically used by masons and other craftsmen to keep a record of their work. The marks would be made on two parallel sticks, one was retained by the mason and the other by the client, to prevent disagreement.

tie beam: a horizontal roof reinforcement beam at the height of the eaves (see also *collar*).

tracery: a form of decoration used on large windows in Gothic architecture. The tracery is usually restricted to just below the window arch. The stone subdivisions of the windows (medillions) would be developed into elaborate patterns with an underlying geometrical framework. These would be adorned with stained glass.

transhumance: the seasonal movement of livestock to different pastures in different geographic zones, much favoured by nomadic and semi-nomadic societies.

transom: a horizontal bar of wood or stone in a window.

truss: self-supporting triangular framework within a roof which supports other timbers.

voussoirs: wedge-shaped stones forming an arch.

wall plate: horizontal timber along the top of a wall designed to hold the ends of the rafters.

wallwalk: path between parapet/battlements and the roof.

window head: a block at the top of a window which incorporates any tracery that might be present.

yett: a defensive iron grille or gate.

Glossary of Gaelic/Historic Terms

agnatic: related to on the father's side (OED).

aimsher chue: coshering season, when the chieftain visited his clan, receiving the hospitality that was his due.

attainder: judgement of death or outlawry, as a result of treason or felony. The attainted person's estate was forfeited, and they could neither inherit or transmit anything by descent. All civil rights and capacities were lost (OED).

ban-tierna: folkloric term (anglic.) for chieftains wife in the early nineteenth century, see also tierna.

Brehon (Irish: *Breitheamh*): judge of native Irish Law.

buannacht: the billetting of servants or mercenaries.

buannacht bheag: 'a money commutation of billeting rights' (Simms 1987, p. 171).

carucate: an area of land equivalent to that worked by a team of eight oxen in one year.

ceithearn tighe: household guards, chieftain's retinue.

chiefry: lordship, dominion, and the dues owing to that position.

churls (ceorl): an English term used by the sixteenth-century English for the lowest grade of Gaelic society. It originally referred to the lowest grade of Anglo-Saxon freeman.

coinnmeadh: the exaction of free billeting for soldiers and servants, and sometimes their animals too.

coshery: an obligatory banquet provided for the chieftain (and his retinue) by certain tenants, once, twice or four times per year.

cotters/cottar/cottier: a landless peasant occupying a cottage belonging to a farm, in return for labour etc.

creaght (creach): plunder or the booty or plunder from a raid, particularly of livestock. Also refers to a raiding party.

cuid oiche: (angl. 'cuddy'): a night's portion (i.e. hospitality to chieftain and his entourage).

cutting: arbitary taxation by the lord.

derbfine: the leading family in a clan, sharing a common paternal ancestor.

fiants: English legal documents.

gallowglas: (Irish; Gallóglaigh): Scottish mercenaries who fought as heavily-armed foot soldiers.

garrans: working horses, sometimes stolen in raids.

kern: Irish mercenary footsoldiers (Irish: *ceithearn* – a band).

livery: the feudal right to demand of others food, provisions or clothing for one's servants (collated with 'coinnmeadh').

musteron: a tax raised to pay for masons, probably originated in commutation of labour services (as in the 'mustering' of an army).

oireachtas: an assembly, sovereignty, authority.

ollamh: a professional, someone with a skill, e.g. medicine, poetry, law, metalworking.

ollamhnacht: approved as an ollamh by the local lord and usually endowed with land.

ollave (angl. of 'ollamh' [See also 'ollamnacht' entry].

pobal: area/territory of a clan or sept.

rectorial tithes: a percentage of farm earnings or produce which clergy were entitled to take from those living in their parish.

refuge towers: a secular building type peculiar to Cork influenced by contemporary Friary church towers. These are distinguished from 'true' tower houses by their small plan which is square, or nearly square. They slightly pre-date or are contemporary with the earliest tower houses.

righdhamhna: 'king material' – i.e. one of a pool of men eligible by nature of birth and attainment to be king.

rising out: a muster of the clan and vassal clans for war on the chieftain's order. Also refers to the number and type of forces expected of each clan and its *septs*.

sept: a division of a nation or tribe (OED).

slat tighearnuis: a rod used in the inauguration of a lord, literally 'rod of lordship'.

tánaiste (angl. 'tanist'): 'second': one second in rank to the chief, the male relative of the chieftain with the highest standing and accepted throughout the clan as his potential successor; usually a brother. In the tower house period, succession by a son became more common.

taoiseach: 'first' leader, chief, clan chieftain.

tierna (Irish: 'tighearna'): 'lord': this term was still current in folk memory in early-nineteenth century rural Cork (see also ban-tierna).

townland: a sub-division of a parish of no fixed size.

tuath (Angl. 'Tooey'): 'a people', a territory (petty kingdom).

undertaker: the name (without its modern connotations!) given to businessmen, merchants and other adventurers who 'undertook' the expense of settling or 'planting' a loyal (i.e. non-Irish) settlement in return for a grant of the combated Irish lands on which the 'plantation' was to be established.

Bibliography

Abbreviations

JCHAS   Journal of the Cork Historical & Archaeological Society

JRSAI   Journal of the Royal Society of Antiquaries of Ireland

Anon., 'Excursion to Timoleague and Blarney Castle' *Royal Society of Irish Antiquaries,* 5th transactions, series III, no. 23 (1893), p. 340.

Anon., 'Notes and Queries', 'Mrs Jeffreys, of Blarney Castle', *JCHAS*, vol. 1, 2nd series (1895), pp. 82–4

Anon., 'The Jefferyes of Blarney', *JCHAS*, vol. 17 (1911), pp. 35–6

Anon., 'Blarney', *JCHAS*, vol. 18 (1912), pp. 52–3

Anon., 'Captain James Jefferyes of Blarney Castle', *JCHAS*, vol. 20 (1914), pp. 156–8

Anon., 'A French Count Visits Blarney', *The Blarney Annual of Fact and Fancy*, vol. 3 (Blarney, 1951)

Barnard, T. and J. Fenlon (eds.), *The Dukes of Ormonde 1610–1745* (Woodbridge 2000)

Beckett, J.C., *A Short History of Ireland* (London, 1981)

Bennett, B.L., *The History of Bandon* (Cork, 1869)

Black, A. and C. (publishers), *Black's Picturesque Tourist of Ireland* (Edinburgh, 1857)

Brewer, J.N., *The Beauties of Ireland*, vol. 2 (London, 1826)

Burke J. and Sir B., *Burke's Genealogical and Heraldic History of the Peerage, Baronetage and Knightage*, 105th edn, ed. Peter Townsend (London, 1970)

Burke, Sir B. *Burke's Genealogical and Heraldic History of the Landed Gentry of Ireland,* 4th edn, ed. L.G. Pine (London, 1958)

Butler, W.F.T., 'The Barony of Muskerry', *JCHAS*, vol. 16, (1910), pp. 81–8; 120–7

Cairns, C.T., *Irish Tower Houses: A County Tipperary case study*, (Group for the Study of the Irish Historic Settlement, Atlone, 1987)

Carr, J., *The Stranger in Ireland* (London, 1805)

Coleman, J., 'Stray Notes on Some Castles of the County of Cork', *JCHAS*, vol. 1, 2nd series (1895), pp. 20–30

Collins, J.T., 'The Last McCarthy of Blarney Castle', *The Blarney Annual of Fact and Fancy*, vol. 3 (Blarney, 1951), pp. 19–21

——'Blarney: Its Story to 1600 A.D.', *Blarney Magazine*, vol. 6 (Summer 1953), pp. 15–18

——'Some Mac Carthys of Blarney and Ballea', *JCHAS*, vol. 59 (1954–5), pp. 1–10; 82–8; 60, 1–5; 75–9

Corkery, D., *The Hidden Ireland* (Dublin, 1924; 1990s reprint)

Crawford Woods, C., 'Blarney Castle, Co. Cork, The Double Structure of Its Keep', *JCHAS*, vol. 20 (1896), pp. 337–44

Crofton Croker, T., *Researches in the South of Ireland* (London, 1824)

Cronnelly, R.F., *A History of the Clan Eoghan* (Dublin, 1864)

Cronin, M., 'Work and Workers in Cork City and County', in *Cork History and Society*, ed. P. O'Flanagan and C.G. Buttimer (Dublin, 1993), pp. 721–54

Cruise O'Brien, M. and C., *A Concise History of Ireland* (London, 1972)

D'Alton, I., 'Keeping Faith: An Evocation of the Cork Protestant Character, 1820–1920', in *Cork History and Society*, ed. P. O'Flanagan, and C.G. Buttimer (Dublin, 1993), pp. 755–92

De Breffny, B., *Castles of Ireland* (London, 1977)

—— and R. Ffolliott, *The Houses of Ireland* (London, 1975)

Donnelly, J.S., 'A Contemporary Account of the Rightboy Movement: The John Barter Bennett Manuscript', *JCHAS*, vol. 88 (1983), pp. 1–50

Ellis, S.G., *Tudor Ireland: Crown, Community and the Conflict of Cultures 1470–1603* (London, 1985)

Elmes, R.M., *Catalogue of Irish Topographical Prints and Original Drawings in the National Library of Ireland* (Dublin, 1943, revised M. Hewson, Dublin, 1975)

Fahy, E.M., 'Castle Inch, Co. Cork', *JCHAS*, vol. 62, (1957), pp. 1–13

Fahy, A.M., 'Place and Class in Cork', in *Cork History and Society*, ed. P. O'Flanagan, and C.G. Buttimer (Dublin, 1993), pp. 793–812

Fitzgerald, K., 'Making it happen: From Fortress to Tourist Attraction', *The Graduate* (1999), pp. 14–15

Gibbings, R., *Lovely is the Lee* (London, 1945)

——'The Blarney Stone', *The Blarney Annual of Fact and Fancy*, vol. 3 (Blarney, 1951)

——*Sweet Cork of Thee* (London, 1952)

Gillman, H.W., 'Carrignamuck Castle, County Cork: A Stronghold of the MacCarthys', *JCHAS*, vol. 1, 1st series (1892a), pp. 11–8; 30–7

——'Sir Cormac Mac Teige MacCarthy and the Sept Lands of Muskerry, Co. Cork; with a Historical Pedigree', *JCHAS*, vol. 1, 1st series (1892b), pp. 193–200

——'Castlemore and Connected Castles in Muskerry, Co. Cork', *JCHAS*, vol. 1a, 1st series (1892c), pp. 213–20; 233–42

Grose, D., *The Antiquities of Ireland: A Supplement to Francis Grose*, ed. R. Stalley (Dublin, 1991)

Hart, P., *The IRA and Its Enemies* (Oxford, 1998)

Hillyard, M.P., 'The Rock Close', *Blarney Magazine*, vol. 7 (1954), pp. 70–1

——*Blarney Castle and Rock Close*, 8th edn (Cork, 1959)

Hoek, K. van, 'Cork Profiles No. 1: Sir George Colthurst', *The Blarney Annual*, vol. 1, (Blarney, 1948), p. 25

Hole, S.R., *A Little Tour in Ireland* (London, 1859)

The Irish Fiants of the Tudor Sovereigns, vol. 2 (1558–86) (Dublin, 1994)

Jones, M., G.I. Meiron-Jones, F. Guibal and J.R. Pilcher, 'The Seigneurial Domestic Buildings of Brittany: A Provisional Assessment', *The Antiquaries Journal*, vol. 69 (1989), pp. 73–110

Kavanagh, P.J., *Voices in Ireland: A Traveller's Literary Companion* (London, 1994)

Kennedy, S., 'Coquebert de Montbret in Search of the Hidden Ireland', *JRSAI*, vol. 82 (1952), pp. 62–7

Leask, H.G., *Irish Castles and Castellated Houses* (Dundalk, 1951, repr. 1964)

Lee, G.L., 'Notes on Some Castles of mid-Cork', *JCHAS*, vol. 20 (1914), pp. 57–68, 113–24

Lewis, S., *A Topographical Dictionary of Ireland*, 2 vols. (London, 1837)

Lockett, R., *Irish Pictures* (London, 1888)

Lucas, A.T., *Cattle in Ancient Ireland* (Kilkenny, 1989)

MacCarthy, C.J.F., 'An Antiquary's Note Book 12', *JCHAS*, vol. 95 (1990), pp. 158–64

MacCarthy Glas, D., *The Life and Letters of Florence Mac Carthy Reagh* (London and Dublin, 1867)

——*Historical Pedigree of the Sliochd Feidhlim, the MacCarthys of Gleanacroim* (Exeter, 1880)

MacCarthy-Morrogh, M., *The Munster Plantation: English Migration to Southern Ireland, 1588–1641* (Oxford, 1986)

Mac Suibhne, M., *Famine in Muskerry* (Macroom, 1997)

Mahony, F.S., *The Reliques of Father Prout*, 2 vols. (London, 1836)

Mallory, J.P. and T.E. McNeill, *The Archaeology of Ulster from Colonisation to Plantation* (The Institute of Irish Studies, Queen's University Belfast, 1991)

McCarthy, S.T., *The MacCarthys of Munster: The Story of a Great Irish Sept* (Dundalk, 1922)

McCarthy, W.P., 'The Litigious Earl of Clancarty', *JCHAS*, vol. 70 (1965), pp. 7–13

McGrath, W., 'The Muskerry Light Railway', *The Blarney Annual of Fact and Fancy*, vol. 4 (Blarney, 1952), p. 54

McNeill, T.E., 'Church-Building in 14th-century Ireland and the "Gaelic Revival"', *The Journal of Irish Archaeology*, vol. 3 (1985–6), pp. 61–64

——*Castles in Ireland: Feudal Power in a Gaelic World* (London, 1997)

Monk, J. & R. Tobin (eds.), *Barryscourt Castle: An Architectural Survey* (Barryscourt, 1991)

Mulcahy, J., 'The Diplomatic Career of Captain James Jefferyes, Blarney Castle', *Journal of the Blarney and District Historical Society*, vol. 6 (2002), pp. 7–30

Newham, A.T,, *The Cork and Muskerry Light Railway*, (rev. S.C. Jenkins, Oxford, 1992)

Nicholls, K., 'Gaelic Society and Economy', in *A New History of Ireland*, ed. A. Cosgrove, (Oxford, 1993a), pp. 397–438

——'The Development of Lordship in Co. Cork, 1300–1600', in *Cork History and Society*, eds. P. O'Flanagan, and C.G. Buttimer (Dublin, 1993b), pp. 157–212

O'Brien, A.F., 'Politics, Economy and Society: The Development of Cork and the Irish South-Coast Region *c.* 1170 to *c.* 1583', in *Cork History and Society*, eds. P. O'Flanagan, and C.G. Buttimer, (Dublin, 1993)

Ó Danachair, C., 'Irish Tower Houses and Their Regional Distribution', *Bealoideas*, vols. 45–7 (1977–9), pp. 158–63

O'Donovan, J., *The Annals of the Kingdom of Ireland by the Four masters from the earliest period to 1616*, 7 vols. (Dublin, 1851)

O'Donovan, J., *The Tribes of Ireland: A Satire*, by Aengus O'Daly (Dublin, 1852)

O'Hart, J., *Irish Landed Gentry* (Dublin, 1887)

——*Irish Pedigrees: Or, the Origin and Stem of the Irish Nation*, vol. 1 (Dublin, 1892)

O'Hegarty, R.S., 'The Blarney Tram', *The Blarney Annual*, vol. 2 (Blarney, 1950), pp. 22–3

O'Mahony, J., *The Sunny Side of Ireland: How to See It from the Great Southern and Western Railway* (Dublin, 1898)

O'Mahony, M., *Famine in Cork City* (Cork, 2005)

Ó Murchadha, D., *Family Names of County Cork* (Dun Laoghaire, 1985)

——'Clann Taidhg Ruaidh na Scairte', *JCHAS*, vol. 99 (1994), pp. 32–46

Otway-Ruthven, A.J., *A History of Medieval Ireland* (repr. New York, 1993)

O'Shea, K., 'A Castleisland Inventory, 1590', *Journal of the Kerry Historical and Archaeology Society*, vols. 15–16 (1982–3), p. 37–46

Pettit, S., *Blarney Castle: The Story of a Legend* (Cork, 1989)

Power, D. (ed.), *Archaeological Inventory of County Cork*, vol. 2 (East and South Cork), (Dublin, 1994)

——*Archaeological Inventory of County Cork*, vol. 3 (Mid Cork), (Dublin, 1997)

Quin, E.G. (ed.), *Dictionary of the Irish Language*, (compact ed), (Dublin, 1990)

Records of Ireland 15th report of Record Commissioners (Abstract 1665 patent) (March 1825)

Reilly, R., 'The Blarney Mills', *The Blarney Annual*, vol. 1 (Blarney, 1948), pp. 33–6

Rose, J., *The Drawings of John Leech*, (London, 1950)

Scarisbrick, J.J., *Henry VIII* (Harmondsworth, 1972)

Simms, K., 'Warfare in Medieval Gaelic Ireland', *Irish Sword*, vol. 12 (1975), pp. 98–108

——'Guesting and Feasting in Gaelic Ireland' *Proc. RAI*, vol. 108 (1978), pp. 67–100

——*From Kings to Warlords: The Changing Political Structure of Gaelic Ireland in the Later Middle Ages* (Woodbridge, 1987)

Stafford, Sir T., *Pacata Hibernia*, 2 vols., ed. S. O'Grady, (London, 1896)

Stanihurst, R., *De rebus in Hibernia gestis libris iv*, (Antwerp, 1584)

Sweetman, D., *Medieval Castles of Ireland* (Cork, 1999)

The Tourist's Illustrated Hand-Book for Ireland, 8th edn. (London, 1860)

Ward Lock and Co. (publishers), *Guide to Cork, Cobh, Glengariff, Killarney and the South-West of Ireland* (London and Melbourne, *c.* 1950)

Windele, J., *Historical and Descriptive Notices of the City of Cork and Its Vicinity* (Cork, 1839)

Wright, G.N., *Ireland Illustrated* (London, 1831).

Young, A., *Arthur Young's Tour in Ireland, 1776–1779*, 2 vols., ed. A.W. Hutton, (London, 1892)

Unpublished Sources

Colthurst, Sir G.V.C. Baronet, photocopy of family tree, (Cork Archives Institute, U196 Colthurst Estate Papers)

Donnelly, C.J., *The Tower Houses of County Limerick*, unpublished PhD thesis, (1994)

Fitzgerald, J., *The Romance of Blarney Castle: Souvenir for Tourists Containing All Items of Interest, from A.D. 1200 to 1897*, unpublished manuscript (1899) (Cork City Library, 941.95)

Harden, J., 'A Tour in Ireland by John Harden in 1797', a diary of the tour, ed. M. Quane

Jordan, J.A., *The Tower Houses of County Wexford*, unpublished PhD thesis, (1991)

McKenna, M., *Evidence for the Use of Timber in Medieval Irish Tower Houses*, unpublished MA thesis, (1984)

Mulcahy, J., *Blarney and District in Troubled Times* (in prep.)

Neill, K.A., *The Manor of Knockgraffon*, unpublished MA thesis, (1983)

O'Malley, E, notebooks (University College Dublin, UCD P17b/112)

Osman, C., 'The Turkish Baths of Cork', draft report 1988. Held by Colthurst family

Phelan, J., The Cork and Muskerry Light Railway, Lecture given to the Blarney and District Historical Society, 6 November 1997

Samuel, M.W., *The Tower Houses of West Cork*, unpublished PhD thesis, (1998)

Simms, K., 'Native Sources for Gaelic Settlement: The House Poems', lecture handout for the Group for the Study of Historic Settlement conference, Settlement and Landscape in Gaelic Ireland (1999)

Newspapers

The Irish Times, 'Final Notice to Claimants and Incumbrances', 9 June 9 1909

Cork Examiner, 'A New Oasis in Ireland' 7 June 1847

'Inniscarra', 5 November 1847

Index

O'Shea, Father, 62–3
Ossian cycle, 66
O'Sullivan Bere, Donal, 43
O'Sullivans, 24
oubliette, 93

Pacata Hibernia, 1, *2*, 11, 42, 87
parapets, 83, 86, 88, 110–16
Payne, Sir Richard, 53
Penn, Sir William, 50
Pettit, S., 67
poets, 9, 10, 16, 52, 72, 118
Poor Relief, 59
Portland, Earl of, 53
Preston, Thomas, 47
Priest's Chamber, 105, *107, 108*
Primrose League, 62, 74
prison, 87
'Prout, Father' (Francis Mahony), 59, 65, 67, 68, 71–2

quarry, 84

Radcliffe, Ann, 66
rafters, 121
railways, 73–6, 78
Raleigh, Sir Walter, 39, 43, 60
rebellion of 1641, 46–9
Reformation, 34
refuge towers, 129
Restoration, 49
Richard II, King, 26
righdhamhna, 4–5
Rightboys, 55–7, 61
Rinuccini, Archbishop, 48
Robinson, John, 54
Roche, Catherine de la, 25
Roche family, 26, 29, 39
Rock Close, 65–6, 68
Rokeby, Sir Thomas de, 24, 25
Romanticism, 65–6, 71, 73
Ross, Bishops of, 10
Rosscarbery, 11–12, 14
Russia, 54

St Anne's Hill, 74–5
St Leger, Sir Anthony, 32–4
St Leger, Sir Warham, 36
Scott, Sir Walter, 66, 72–3
septs, 4, 7, 11, 23

settlement, 11, 14
Settlement, Act of, 49, 60
Shane, 60
Sheriff of Cork, 36
Sherrard, Mr, 74
Shournagh River, 3, 77, 78
sickroom, 125
Sidney, Sir Henry, 36
Sidney, Sir Philip, 39
Simms, K., 5, 6, 7, 71, 72
Simnel, Lambert, 29
Sinn Féin Club, 63
Sournagh valley, 65
south wall, 90–1, *92*
Spencer, Elizabeth (Countess Clancarty), 50, 51, 53
Stafford, Sir T., 1, *2*, 87, 98
stairs, 106
    Black Stairs, 101, 126
    main spiral stair, 119
Stanihurst, Richard, 6, 18
station, 73, 76, 78
Statutes of Kilkenny, 25
storeroom, 98–9
Strafford, Lord, 46
'surrender and regrant', 31, 45
Surrey, Earl of, 31
Sweden, 54
Sweeneys, 9
Sweet, Mr, 53

tánaiste (tanist), 5, 27
taoiseach (chieftains), 4–5, 7
tapestries, 101
taxation, 19
Taylor, Harriet, 60
Thomond, Earl of, 45
Timoleague, 14
Tipperary, 14, 19
Togher, 16, 134
tourism, 65–76
tower houses, 6, 14–20, 26–8
    defence of, 10, 11, 15, 17
    design of, 15–17, 129–33
    halls, 16–17, 18
    payment for and upkeep, 18–19
    refuge towers, 129
Trant, Dominick, 57
turret, 112, 115, 133
Tyrone, Hugh O'Neill, Earl of, 39–40, 41, 43